MW00453203

Money Matters

Everything You Should Have Learned in School, but Didn't

Your Guide to Personal Financial Success from The Beginning

Written By: Veronica Karas, CFP®

ISBN: 978-1-54396-004-4

Gratitude & Dedication

Thank you to every single person who contributed questions, topics, and general ideas for this book.

Thank you to my clients of the last 10+ years for helping me to tell a better story.

Thank you to my three bosses for everything you have taught me.

Thank you to my amazing friends and family for all your love and support.

Thank you to my incredible husband for all you do to make every aspect of our lives absolutely incredible. Also, thank you for listening to all my meadow reports.

Most importantly, thank you to my Mom.

Mom, thank you for making me the person I am today. Thank you for showing me what strength, determination, and courage looks like.

Thank you for your unconditional love.

This book is for you.

Table of Contents

"It is well enough that people of the nation do not understand our banking and monetary system, for if they did, I believe there would be a revolution before tomorrow morning."
-Henry Ford

CONGRATULATIONS! Please take a moment to pause and celebrate yourself. You are taking a massive leap forward in your life and, after you finish this book, you will have all the tools you need to make outstanding financial decisions every single day for the rest of your life!

This book is for you if:

1. You feel like you could have a better understanding of how to manage your money that is congruent with your goals.

2. You're like the average kid in America and you never learned how to manage your money.

3. You're a parent who wants to help educate your kids, so that they can excel in every area of their lives, including their finances.

4. You're a recent college graduate and you want to get started on the right track – financially.

5. You're graduating high school and want to know how to build a solid financial foundation.

6. You're working on getting your financial house in order.

7. You want to learn more about finances and integrate healthier financial habits into your life.

I run into so many people these days that are just confused about everything going on with their finances. Many of these people happen to be close friends and family, and I'm determined to help.

I'm here to clear everything up. My personal mission is to help young professionals take control of their financial lives – creating a "pay yourself first" system, avoiding unnecessary costs, asking better questions, and becoming empowered through knowledge. By reading this book, you will learn so much about all aspects of personal finance that you will become a resource among your group of friends for all things financial, regardless of what you do for a living. It's a lofty goal.

To be quite honest, I'm tired of our generation dealing with so much debt and so few assets. I'm tired of hearing that my 30-year-old friends are struggling to figure out how to pay rent this month because they don't understand how to maximize their savings and minimize their costs. I know way too many objectively successful people who are being swallowed whole by their school loans, and credit card debt. I'm here to turn the tide around, and help you stop googling for financial advice in the process. I may use some strong language to describe various elements of financial planning. Please know that this is intentional. Nothing is as effective as the word "FUCK" in waking me up and I hope that I can share the same benefit with you.

Let's all be honest here:

Between bankers, planners, brokers, attorneys, accountants, and 17 other professionals – you could easily spend more money than you probably have in your bank just trying to find the right advice. We don't learn personal finance in school and the world just serves to confuse us more the longer we spend in it. The other unspoken thing is that everyone thinks their method, or their plan, is the best way or the only way. The truth about finance is that there is a lot of "gray" area. There are multiple solutions to every problem. There are multiple pathways to every outcome.

One rule: we're officially best friends. You can reach out to me, ask me questions, ask for advice, and we can most definitely meet and hang out in the real world, and in return, all I ask is that you share anything you find valuable in this book with all the people you know and love. Bonus points if you buy them a copy!

With that said, please allow me to introduce myself.

As I sit here and write this book, I am home, in Port Washington, NY. I'm 28 years old and have worked in the Financial Services industry for just about ten years. I started by working for a life insurance company, then spent about six months working for a large investment research firm. I was then lucky enough to get hired to work as a full-time marketing associate for a small Registered Investment Advisor (RIA). While working at the RIA, I began to sit in on client meetings and getting to know everyone we worked with.

Clients started to come to me with their questions since I was in their meetings, and I became interested in pursuing the CERTIFIED FINANCIAL PLANNER™ designation (yes, they make us write it in all CAPS like that). I earned that designation in 2012 and have since been working directly with individuals from all walks of life, helping them to get their financial house in order, minimize their tax burden, maximize their savings and investment earnings, organize their estate planning, figure out what kind of insurance and how much they need, and everything else that touches their financial lives. I've paid bills for clients, purchased boats and cars for clients, helped them sell their homes, helped them buy the home of their dreams, helped them send their kids to college, planned their dream trips, and planned their retirement. Amid this time, I spent about eight months working for a large brokerage firm – a disaster of an experience that didn't align with my personal moral compass. I went running right back to the RIA world where I genuinely feel blessed to be every single day.

I have worked with ultra-high-net worth individuals, individuals with loads of debt, individuals who never had money and are suddenly inheriting a boat load, and basically everyone in between. The one common denominator is that most people have no idea what they are doing or why. Most people don't even ask the right questions. Do you know how empowering this book would be if it was just a list of amazing questions to ask various professionals? That alone would be priceless, because when you ask better questions, you get better answers! How many people would benefit from having better answers in their lives?

I'm so thrilled to be able to serve and help so many people, and I love what I get to do every single day. More importantly: I believe, with every fiber of my being, that I have been put on this planet to free people from financial pain and struggle.

To that end, I hope this book will serve as the bridge between everything you learned in school and everything you should have learned. I hope it takes you to new places and opens new doors simply because you will have more knowledge and ask better questions.

Let's start a new generation of financially-savvy, outstanding, and empowered professionals!

I love you. Thank you.

Veronica K.

Chapter 1

Where Do I Start?

"Beware of Little Expenses, A Small Leak Will Sink a Great Ship"

- Benjamin Franklin

This is, by far, the most common question I get as a Financial Planner. The answer is always the same (and people always respond in the most begrudged fashion I have ever seen): Figure out what your spending is.

If you're sitting there and you're about to put this book down because you mentally just started calculating how much of your money goes to Starbucks or Chipotle or Sephora, then I would strongly encourage you to push through. This is by far the most difficult part of financial planning and there is no way to avoid it.

Most younger people I've spoken to strongly prefer to spend their money on experiences - travel, Broadway shows, sky diving, etc.- but they don't have the money to do it because they've spent everything they have buying fancy coffee and "stuff". It's the little things you spend money on that cost the most in the long run.

As an example, let's say you spend $5 on a wonderful latte coffee every single day of the work week (Monday to Friday). Seems innocent enough. That would be $25 per week. On average there are 50 work weeks in a year so that would equate to spending $1,250 per year on coffee. Again, seems simple enough. Let's say that instead of putting it towards coffee, you put that amount into your investment account each year, at a reasonable compounding rate of return of just 5%.

At the end of 10 years you would have $16,242.63

At the end of 20 years you would have $42,994.41

At the end of 30 years you would have $87,054.83

At the end of 40 years (the length of a typical working career) you would have $159,622.77

There are literally places in the United States where you can buy a beautiful home for $160,000. $160,000 is enough to cover the cost of 4 years of college at a state school. $160,000 is enough to cover 16 years of really nice travel and trips. For $160,000 you could take an annual trip around the entire world for 6 years straight and still have money left over. However, you decided to piss that money away (literally) on fancy coffee.

I promise that I'm not using this example to scare you, I'm using it to show you that everything you spend money on today is money that you will not have available for spending in the future. You want to make sure, as early on as possible, that your spending aligns with your priorities. By figuring out where you spend your money, and being honest about it, you can also figure out how to reallocate your money to places that may better serve you. For instance, if you're spending $1,250 on coffee each year, maybe you can cut that in half by purchasing an in-home coffee maker, and then have $625 each year to spend on a trip, an upgrade to first class on your next flight, or contribute to your retirement account. Let's jump right into how to figure out your budget.

Listing your income and expenses (or your budget) is going to be a simple process but really take the time and energy to make it thoughtful. Start with listing out all your fixed expenses. There are things you absolutely must pay for in order to live. If you lost your job, these expenses would not go away and cannot be eliminated. Some common examples are:

- Rent/ Maintenance/Mortgage/ Homeowner's Association fees
- Utilities
  - Electric
  - Gas
  - Water
  - Telephones – cell phone/landline
- Insurance Premiums
  - Health
  - Auto
  - Homeowners
  - Life
  - Disability
- Childcare related expenses (if any)
- Medical care, food, a basic amount of clothing, diapers, etc.
- Minimum payments on any loans or outstanding debt
- Ongoing home maintenance expenses, such as repairs

After you have figured those out, now it's time to list out all of your variable expenses. These are expenses that change with time and depend on your circumstances. If you lost your job, these would be the expenses you could eliminate or minimize to reduce the cost of your lifestyle. For this, you will want to make sure you have two columns. Label the first one "current" and the second one "goals". For this exercise, really focus on the "current" column and figuring out exactly what you spend in each category. Be as honest and real as possible, even if the numbers on the page seem unrealistic. Some common variable expenses are:

- Food expenses
    - Breakfast
    - Coffee
    - Lunch
    - Snacks
    - Groceries
    - Dinners
- Child care expenses
    - Those related to activities and sports like piano lessons
    - Nanny/day care
    - Allowances
- Clothing
- Laundry service/Dry cleaning
- Subscriptions
- Memberships
- Gifts

- Donations/Charity

- Personal Care

- Barber/Beauty Shop

- Toiletries

- Spa/Massage

- Travel

- Beer/Wine/Liquor

- Entertainment

- Pet Care/Supplies

- Hobbies/Crafts

Once you're done figuring out both your fixed and variable expenses, add the numbers together.

Now, find your last few pay stubs or check your bank account for the checks that get auto-deposited into it and figure out how much your net pay (the amount you get paid after taxes) is each month. Subtract the number you got for all your expenses from the amount of pay you receive. There are 3 possible outcomes here: The number is positive, the number is negative, or the number is zero.

If the number is positive - this means you're saving money each month. Does the number you calculated match the dollar amount of money you have saved? If not, go back and figure out what you're not counting. It is extremely important to be as accurate as possible. If you're off by a few dollars, that is fine; it's likely cash that you're spending and not accounting for. If you're off by a significant amount, then figure out where the money goes since it must be going somewhere. Fortunately for all of us, money does not just disappear into thin air.

If the number you have is negative – this means you are spending more than you earn. Take some time and re-evaluate your spending. Where can you cut back and cut back right now? Do you order out or go to nice dinners often? Maybe you're too charitable. Maybe you can stay home a few more nights per week. You need to do the work to figure out how to live within the income you make or immediately find a way to increase your income. This is the red zone; the danger zone. You want to make sure you're living within your means because not doing so means debt. It also usually means credit card balances and large interest rates that should be avoided.

If the number is zero – this means you currently live paycheck-to-paycheck. It is likely that you can cut back in a few places and get into the positive side to start saving.

If you have made it this far and have done the work, then CONGRATU-LATIONS! You're officially ahead of the 85% of people I've spoken to that have no clue what they spend and how much their lifestyle costs. If you're reading this and have simply chosen to glaze over this and convince yourself that this exercise is not for you, then I encourage you to go back and do it anyway. Most people are shocked by the amount they spend on seemingly frivolous or useless things. How much is your landline costing you each month and when is the last time you used it? I used coffee as an example of frivolous spending but honestly there are so many things. As a part-time yoga instructor, there was a point where I managed to accumulate 50 pairs of leggings. I wore about 5 of them at any given time and the rest just used up valuable closet real-estate in my home.

Knowing where your money goes is the first step towards financial freedom. It may seem ridiculous to count every single dollar, but the more dollars you accumulate, the wealthier you become. One of the most eye-opening lessons I had early on in my career is realizing that the wealthiest clients were the ones who were extremely careful about where they spent their money. They saved large chunks of everything they made so they can create an abundant future for themselves and their family.

If you're in your 20's now and single or dating, then take a moment to realize that your life will only get more expensive from here. Houses are more expensive to maintain than apartments. Children come with seemingly never-ending expenses that also increase. Going out to dinner or traveling with your friends may seem like it's pretty expensive now, but at some point in your life you may begin to plan a trip to Disney for you, your spouse, and your two kids, and then you will think back to the days where your biggest concern was making sure you can pay your measly $1,500 in rent. Disney family trips are beyond expensive, in fact, and you should probably start saving for them now.

The next thing you want to do is figure out what your goals actually are. What are you trying to do with your money? What do you wish you had the money to be able to afford to do now? Write these down! Make it the craziest, most robust, and most exciting list you have ever made.

Below is some of my personal list so you can get an idea of what I really mean by making a list of everything you want to be able to do. The reality is that all goals cost money. It's just a matter of how much money you're willing to save based on how much each goal excites you. My goals are:

1. Buy a six-bedroom home with two acres of land

2. Own an Alpaca farm

3. Fund a dog shelter

4. Publish five books

5. Own a vacation home in the Poconos

6. Travel four times per year

7. Become a Tony Robbins Trainer

8. Complete Tony Robbins' Business Mastery course

Clearly, I have a passion for animals and personal development. Honestly, looking at this list not only encourages me to save money, but it also encourages me to hustle my ass off to reach my career goals. One of the biggest goals that most young people strive for is to buy their first home.

Owning a home used to be a virtual requirement in attaining the so-called American dream. But that was when people drove two-ton cars, smoked on airplanes and watched live television. Buying is a smart choice for many people, but it isn't always the best deal, depending on the market where you live and other factors. Such as how long you plan to stay in your home and the size of the home you want to purchase compared to where you're renting.

Before you commit to buying, factor in the following points:

- There is a big initial investment involved. You must come up with a lot of money when you purchase your house, from the closing costs (roughly 3% of the home's purchase price) to the down payment itself. Not everyone has that kind of cash to spare. Especially not when you're just getting started in your financial life. It may or may not be worthwhile to decide that you want to live with your parents for a few more years in order to save up to buy a home but that could be a problematic decision for many.

- Can you handle the debt? Lenders often look at your debt-to-income ratio: how your mortgage payments and other debts would stack up against your pay. Conventional lenders often use the so-called 28/36 rule when determining whether to offer you a mortgage loan. Your house-related payments (i.e.: mortgages, taxes, and insurance) should not exceed 28% of your pretax income, and all other combined debts, such as revolving credit card loans, car loans, or school loans, should not exceed 36% of your monthly pretax income.

- Buying is more expensive than you think. You cannot simply compare your monthly mortgage payment to your monthly rent — these are apples and oranges, particularly when you consider that the place you purchase will not necessarily be the same size as the place you're renting. Though you can deduct some of your home-ownership expenses, you will have to pay property taxes, homeowner's insurance, HOA fees and maybe primary mortgage insurance, as well as renovations, maintenance, utilities, and other fees that are not your responsibility if you rent.

- Buying decreases ease of mobility. In today's ever-changing job market, very few people can say with certainty that they'll have the same employer in five years. It's much easier, and less expensive, to leave a yearlong lease than to sell a home.

- How hot is your market? Real estate is local and cyclical, so consider whether your area is better suited to renting or buying. If you live in a large metropolitan area, the Case-Shiller Index provides a useful glance at how current real estate values where you live compare to historic highs and lows.

Is buying a home an investment or an expense?

Some people would rather put their money toward equity in their property instead of giving it to a landlord. While that math makes sense for many — especially those who plan to stay long enough to pay off their mortgage entirely — nobody can predict whether home prices will rise or fall in a given time frame, so don't count on your home to be a cash cow.

If you're thinking about buying, follow these steps before making your move.

1. Calculate your current debts, including car loans, credit card payments, and student loans. Remember the 28/36 rule mentioned above.

2. Consider how much available cash you have. You will want enough to at least cover your down payment and closing costs, and don't forget to leave enough in your bank account to cover any emergencies that might arise.

3. Make sure you can put enough money down. Traditionally, lenders have required down payments equal to 20% of the home's purchase price, but special programs allowing down payments as low as 3% are available. (Putting 20% down on a $300,000 home

would require $60,000 in the bank - plus an additional $9,000 or so for closing costs.)

4. Get pre-approved for a loan. Contact a lender to get pre-approved for a mortgage. This does not require you to accept the loan; it's just a way of showing real estate agents and sellers that you're serious. One of the first things a prospective agent will ask is whether you have been pre-approved, so check this box off early in the process.

Should I just keep renting?

Deciding whether to rent or buy is a big decision that requires serious "Where am I now?" and "Where am I going?" sorts of questions. It might be best to keep renting if you want to maintain maximum flexibility for personal or professional reasons, or if jumping into more debt right now takes you out of your comfort zone. Maybe you're just not ready to face the responsibilities of home-ownership: repairs, upgrades, maintenance, yard-work and all the rest. Even thinking about the difference between cleaning an 800-square-foot apartment and a 2,400-square-foot house can make you want to take a seat and a deep breath.

Your local housing market could be working against you, as well. If you live in a hot market with eager house hunters chasing too few properties, it might be best to wait until a better buying opportunity presents itself. However, the biggest and most important thing to remember is that a home you own is an asset on your balance sheet for as long as you choose to keep it. It is something you could sell if things get really tough. It is also something you can pass down to your children. Even if you never pay off the mortgage on your house, it is still forever an asset that you own and an asset that you can liquidate. Yes, it would take time to sell your home, and it can be expensive to do so, but keep in mind that those who rent are paying someone else's mortgage. You can be one of those people whose mortgages gets paid by renting out your home, or even a part of your home.

As a note, although it can get expensive to own a home, a lot of it depends on the type of person you are. Some people really enjoy doing fix-up projects or are handy, which is a huge cost savings, especially over time. On the other hand, those who are not so handy, will not see such a benefit and the costs of paying someone to do all your housework for you can add up quite quickly. Plus, you would have the added frustration of dealing with various vendors and workers, which probably makes you pretty unhappy with your new home-owning responsibilities.

There is a reason that it's a common American dream - because it honestly feels amazing to be building equity in a house that you own.

Chapter 2

Pay Yourself First

"A Penny Saved is A Penny Earned"

-Benjamin Franklin

Now that you have done your budget, hopefully you have realized you're saving money or could adjust your spending to start saving money. You will need to be have some wiggle room in your budget for this to work.

Very often I find people get into their 30's, 40's, 50's and even 60's and no one bothered to teach them the one key habit that could change their financial lives.

It is the concept of *pay yourself first.*

The mistake that most people make is that they hope they have money left over in their bank accounts after they've done all their spending. So they will have paid their rent, bought groceries, ordered half their meals through seamless, thrown their groceries out, and bought some new shoes, and then they have $25 left at the end of the month and they call that "savings".

The real power of creating wealth and abundance in your life comes from saving money upfront.

Every time you get a paycheck, put your savings aside, into a separate account, hopefully where it will not seem as accessible for you as spending money. This way, if you end up spending too much in a specific month, it's not your savings that takes the hit, it's your eating out habits. Essentially, the order in which you spend the money you earn matters and it should go something like this:

1. Receive income

2. Move specific/planned amount to savings

3. Pay all fixed expenses

4. Spend the rest of it however you originally planned

5. Move anything left over at the end of the month to savings (consider this a bonus to yourself).

The way you stop living paycheck-to-paycheck and built a nest egg, an emergency fund, a college savings fund, a retirement fund, a dream house fund, and a million other things – including becoming a millionaire, is to get into the habit of paying yourself first.

On that note, I often get asked, why in the world do I need to save money anyway? You need money to sustain your lifestyle for a prolonged period of time. Aside from death being an awful financial plan, here are a few other reasons you may want to save money:

- Retirement

   o There will likely be a significant and lengthy period of time in your life when you are not bringing home the cheddar. If you are earning $100,000 a year now and spending all of it, I assure you that there is no government program out there that will support your lifestyle. So, unless you are ready to dramatically reduce your lifestyle when you're 70 years old, you will want to start working on this as early in life as possible.

- Home(s)

  o Renting is cute and all but honestly, part of the big American dream for most people is to own a home. You don't want to be 80 years old and fighting with your landlord or risking being evicted because they are destroying the building you live in to build shiny new condos. Seriously, this happens. You need to save money to have a down payment to buy a house.

- Emergency Fund (probably should be #1 if I had to pick one)

  o Shit happens in life and you need to be able to pay for said shit. Sometimes literally, like when the main sewer line of your bathroom is clogged and there is shit coming out of your shower drain. I don't know about you, but I cannot (and really don't want to) fix that. Not having an emergency fund is a huge reason why people get into debt in the first place. Unforeseen medical expenses, for instance, are the current number one cause of bankruptcy in the United States. Building an emergency fund in advance can help prevent you from getting into financial trouble if something comes up.

  o As a general note, everyone should have three to six months of expenses in cash. In case you lose your job or want the ability to change careers because your coworker is a miserable old hag that you can no longer stand. You will need to pay the bills and sustain yourself and you don't want to get into debt while dealing with an employment gap, nor do you want to live in a box under the bridge during that time.

- Travel

    o This adds to the list of things you may want to do without getting into debt. For me, personally, this is on my top three. I believe travel makes us richer, unless it quite literally makes us bankrupt. However, it would be silly to ignore that most travel comes with a hefty price tag. Even if you're traveling to a developing country, it often costs a lot to get there. Between plane tickets, hotels, and all the eating out involved in a trip, it's something that you need to plan for, and budget for, in advance.

- Debt

    o There is nothing sexy about carrying toxic credit card debt. If you're in it, get out as fast as you possibly can, and find a way to save money despite having the debt. If an emergency happens, you probably want to avoid getting further into debt. Pay yourself first no matter what debt you have!

- Financial Freedom (an ultimate goal for many)

    o If you woke up in the morning, and time and money were not an obstacle for you – what would you be doing? Unlimited time. Unlimited money. Whatever that is, figure out how much it would cost you to do it every day of your life and save towards that. What is better than saving towards your dream life? I like to call this "Fuck you money". As in, you can wake up any day and say FUCK

YOU to wherever you're supposed to be and whoever you're supposed to see just because you can.

I take my goal to have full financial freedom very seriously and it keeps me motivated to save and invest money any chance that I get. Here are a few of my "tricks" for saving money:

- Put aside each five-dollar bill into a box every time you get one. Do not spend your fives. Deposit the money at the end of each year into your investment account.

- Set up an auto deposit from your paycheck to a bank that isn't the bank where you have your checking account, so you cannot see that this money is available unless you went looking for it.

- Eat out one time less each week.

- Bring your lunch to work with you and don't order in.

- Don't spend any money at coffee shops (it is most definitely the little things that add up). Your $12 salads during lunch are also making a huge impact. The cost of eating out is typically two to four times that of preparing it yourself.

- Buy less stuff. Really think about everything you buy and ask yourself if you love it. Some things are worth purchasing, but other things end up collecting dust in the back corner of your closet.

- Sell clothing and other items that you have not used or worn in the last year. Invest the proceeds instead of replacing those items.

I often get asked "Bench-marking" questions. For instance: "I'm 30 years old, what should I have saved by now?"

Here is a neat and simple break down to help you stay on track:

First of all, every single person should have at least three to six months of their expenses in cash or cash-like equivalents. This is your emergency fund and it is incredibly important for the general stability of your financial plan to have this in place.

Second, as soon as you start working, you should contribute to your company's available retirement plan, and save about 15% of your income between retirement plan savings and your own personal savings.

Lastly, before I dole these targets out for you. All of the numbers below assume that you are living within your means or, said in a different way you are not spending more than you earn.

The Milestones:

- Age 30 - The goal is to have one times your gross salary saved. If you make $100,000 you should have saved about $100,000 by now.

- Age 35 - Have two times salary saved

- Age 40 - Have three times salary saved

- Age 50 - Have six times salary saved

- Age 60 - Have eight times salary saved

- Age 67 (current average US retirement age) - Have ten times salary saved

There are a few key assumptions in this that are worth noting:

- You will meet these goals if you start saving 15% of your income on an annual basis starting at age 25.

- You invest at least 50% of your savings in stocks (equities) on average over your lifetime.

- You retire at age 67. If you retire later, you will need to have less money saved. If you wish to retire sooner, then the opposite is true.

Another way to look at savings is using the three buckets strategy. I'm trying to provide an abundance of options for you since figuring out a way to save money that makes sense for you and is easy to stick with, is arguably the most important decision you will ever make.

The three buckets strategy also happens to be a strategy for managing money over a multi-year period and helps you to apply an appropriate asset allocation for money you will need in a few months, a few years, in 10 years or more. Here is how it generally works:

- Bucket 1: This bucket typically holds one- or two-years' worth of living expenses, invested in traditionally more stable vehicles such as cash, certificates of deposit, money-market funds, or short-term bonds. Putting money you plan to spend soon into liquid, generally low-volatility investments can help you avoid having to sell riskier investments, such as stock, during a down market to raise cash for living expenses. This bucket should be refilled annually if it gets used.

- Bucket 2: This typically holds money that you expect to need within three to ten years, invested in intermediate-term assets with a focus on growth and capital preservation. This would be a healthy mix of stocks and bonds, usually invested about 50/50 from the start and slowly made more conservative over time as you get closer to needing it.

- Bucket 3: This bucket typically holds money that you expect to need in ten years or later, invested for growth and income. This would be the most aggressively allocated bucket of the three since the fluctuations in your investments will not have a drastic impact on your short or intermediate-term goals.

There are lots of other ways to use buckets, depending on where you are in life. If you're in your 20s, consider one bucket for your emergency fund, another earmarked for a down payment on a home in a few years, and a third invested for retirement. As you move through life, buckets can be used to save money for a child's college tuition, a new car, or a once-in-a-lifetime vacation. Even retirement accounts can be invested in multiple ways. For example, some investors have opened separate IRAs- one for their personal use, invested based on their risk tolerance and investment timeframe; and the other for their children to inherit, which may be invested more aggressively to suit a longer timeframe and higher risk tolerance.

Ultimately, any savings strategy will work if you're saving money. I encourage everyone I know to pay themselves first, and if you get nothing else from this book, I hope you take that advice and action it immediately.

One of the very first clients I started working with, let's call her Lisa, was a school teacher her whole life her and her husband was a principal. They both lived in New York City, earning modest salaries for their respective professions. They went on two modest vacations every year, had one child who they helped in every way possible, but mostly they focused on building their retirement nest egg. They saved everything they could and fully utilized the awesome teacher retirement plan system that is offered to teachers in New York City. Because they were super focused on making sure their retirement was safe and sound, they were able to retire with over $3,000,000 in investment savings. Yes, you read that correctly, three million dollars. At the time of her retirement, Lisa was 65 years old, the mortgage was paid off on their apartment, she was ready to start living her life, giving her time away by volunteering in inner-city schools, and she had three million dollars to go and enjoy every moment of life.

Let me tell you, most people don't get the pleasure of being able to improve their lifestyles once they retire. It's why you always hear about old people having to downsize. No one wants to be in a position where they must sell their home in order to be able to afford to live, and even more so, no one wants to be in a position where they eventually have to rely on their children for money. Get into the habit of saving money now, before life starts actually getting expensive.

On the bright side, now you have the tools to get it right! All of the strategies in this chapter will help you reach your financial goals, just pick the one that sounds easiest or makes the most sense for you!

Chapter 3

The ABC's of Finance

"The Goal Isn't More Money. The Goal is Living Life on Your Terms"

-Will Rogers

Almost everyone I've spoken to in my fourteen years of being part of the workforce has experienced the same thing. They start a job, they know nothing about money, they get handed a bunch of paper, they get told to do various things and pull various bits of information, and they are crudely unprepared for all of it. Most of my friends and colleagues went home after they got their new job paperwork and asked their parents to explain to them what a bank account was, why they needed one, and how to fill out the forms their new potential boss just gave them. What happens if your parents only know the basics and are not much help when you start going deeper with your questions? If you're anything like me, you started asking people around you, and then hopped on the internet and got to work trying to piece together all the information out there about personal financial planning. Why, in the actual fuck, are we not taught finances in school? I must have learned the Pythagorean theorem for eight semesters straight, and I have not used it a single time in my adult life. But taxes... eyyyy that is something the education system leaves out! I'm not going to get controversial on you or start sharing conspiracy theories right off the bat, but this is a huge personal pain point of mine.

I'm going to work from the foundation here. Let's assume you are just turning 18 and you need to open your first bank account. Maybe you don't even know how a credit card works. Maybe you don't even know why you need to have a credit card or what building credit means. Let's go back to basics – so we can get to where we need to be and make it easy and fun in the process.

First thing first – everyone should have a checking account and likely a savings account. A checking account is a type of bank account in which you can deposit checks and write checks. It is your bank account for every day expenses. Any money you earn will go into it, and any bills you must pay, or cash you need to withdraw, will come out of it. There is no limit to how often you can access your money from this account, and it usually comes with handy features – like the ability to pay bills online through an application or website. I usually tell people to ask their parents where they do their banking and ask them to take you there to open an account. When there is an existing relationship with a bank, the bank tends to give favorable rates, or family rates, on any kinds of fees or minimum balances or deposit amounts. This is super helpful when you're just getting started as fees will eat away very quickly at your earnings, especially in the beginning of your career.

Once you have a checking account, you can easily open a savings account to go with it. A savings account should serve as the place where you stash money away that you don't spend, or that you actively plan on saving towards some short or long-term financial goals. This would be an account that you predominantly transfer money into, often and regularly, and rarely transfer money out of. Savings accounts tend to earn an interest rate, which may be some nominal amount, but over time will help your money grow.

When you deposit money into a bank account or similar account, you are basically lending your money to the bank or financial institution. The bank takes the money you deposit with them and invests it, allowing them to earn money on your money by lending it to other customers – through auto loans, credit cards, or mortgages for example, or by simply re-investing it in interest-bearing securities. As a "thank you," the bank pays you interest on the money you choose to deposit with them. The opposite is true when you borrow money; you would be paying interest on the amount that you borrow from the bank.

An interest rate is a number that describes the cost of the money you borrow, or how much you will earn on your deposits. Rates are usually quoted as an annual rate, so you can figure out how much interest will be due on any amount of money, for a day, week, month, or other period. A bank will pay out less in interest on savings accounts than they charge customers who borrow from them. This is how banks make a large portion of their money.

The Annual percentage Yield (APY) is a term your bank will use on their marketing material and that you will see on your account statement, is how the interest you earn with your bank is typically quoted. The word percentage means "for each one hundred," and as a result you can estimate interest on every hundred dollars you deposit or borrow. For example, a savings account may pay a 2% APY. APY is typically used because it takes compounding (earning interest on top of interest you previously earned) into account. The actual interest rate you earn is often lower than the quoted APY, but after compounding you can earn the full APY. This means that if you leave your money untouched, you should earn a yield, or return, equal to the quoted APY over one year. For example, let's assume your bank pays 2% APY on your savings. For every $100 you have deposited, you can expect to earn $2 over the course of one year.

Annual percentage Rate (APR) is the interest rate that is charged on consumer loans. The number tells you how much you can expect to pay for every year that you use the money you're borrowing. Typically, the APR includes various fees that the bank charges for the privilege you receive of taking a loan out from them. Making sure you know all the costs involved, is super important! You may also notice that your interest rates change, or that you opened a bank account that earns one rate of interest, but your friend has a bank account with a totally different rate. The fact of the matter is that Interest rates change over time, moving higher or lower – sometimes dramatically, for a variety of reasons. A few of these are:

- Economic conditions - when the economy is strong, rates tend to rise (sooner or later)

- Goals of the bank - Lenders will lower rates if they are eager to lend, and banks will raise rates if they are trying to attract more money to the institution

- Borrower risk - borrowers with high credit scores tend to get lower rates

- Loan characteristics - lenders evaluate all aspects of a loan to determine rates, and short-term loans or loans secured by collateral often have lower rates. I promise to dive deeper into what this means later in the book.

Some good questions to ask at the bank when you open an account:

1. What is the minimum deposit and how much do I need to deposit to open the account?

2. Is there a minimum balance that must be kept in this account? If so, what is it?

3. What happens if the balance drops below the minimum?

4. What fees, if any, are associated with the account?

   a. Some typical fees include, but are not limited to:

      i. Overdraft fees - fees charged if your balance in the account drops below $0.

      ii. ATM fees - fees charged for withdrawing money from an ATM not associated with your bank. For instance, if you bank with Chase but went to make a withdrawal at a Bank of America ATM, Bank of America and Chase may both charge you for using the Bank of America ATM instead of a Chase ATM.

      iii. Account Maintenance fees - fees the bank charges for the privilege of providing you a bank account. I would highly suggest finding a bank that does not have these fees - there are so many banking options out there!

iv.   Withdrawal limit fees - Fees for excess number of withdrawals from your savings account.

v.   Bounced check fees - fees charged by the bank if you write a check but don't have the funds to cover the balance of the check.

vi.   Returned deposit fees - if someone writes you a check that you deposit but they don't have the funds to cover the check they wrote so the deposit is cancelled. Your bank may charge a fee for this "inconvenience."

vii.   Additional checks fees - fees charged by the bank for issuing you a new check book. Again, it's very easy to find banks that don't charge this.

viii.   Paper statement fees - banks are really trying to go green and provide only online statements. To encourage people to manage their finances online, they may charge a fee for providing a paper statement.

ix.   Debit card transaction fees - some banks still charge for using your debit card, and you should avoid these banks like a plague!

x.   Lost card fees - if you lose your debit card, they may charge you to replace it

xi. Inactivity fees - banks may charge you for not using your account. Again, please find a different bank.

5. Does the bank offer free overdraft protection? (This means the bank would decline a charge that would drop your balance below $0.)

6. Are there fees associated with closing the account if I ever wanted to?

7. What is the current interest rate and how often is it compounded?

8. When was the last time they increased interest rates? Do they have a time frame for re-evaluating current interest rates?

9. What services are included with opening an account?

10. Are there any additional perks?

11. Do they offer free credit monitoring or support?

12. Why bank with this bank instead of any other? (Whoever you visit at the bank should be able to tell you why they are the absolute best, and it should sound convincing!)

Keep in mind that your bank does not need to be a brick-and-mortar bank. There are plenty of amazing online banks, like Ally Bank or Ever Bank, that often offer much better rates and less fees overall.

As we discuss checking accounts and savings accounts, I think it's important to just note what all the different types of accounts are. It's hard to know what kind of account to open if you don't know what that account is or what that does for you.

Below is a list, albeit a slightly boring one, of some of the most common account types out there and what they do.

- **Checking Accounts** are also known as demand deposit accounts in some places. This is what we covered earlier in this chapter. The user has a checkbook and an ATM card. These accounts are often used to pay bills and draw money from cash machines. Most checking accounts come with a bill pay and transfer function and have some cool online features as well. They come in a variety of colors and flavors, so to speak, and are called things like: basic checking accounts, joint checking accounts, reward checking accounts, student checking accounts, money market checking accounts, to name a few. Sometimes they'll have cool features, such as paying you dividends or interest, which will give you the benefit of higher interest rates like a savings account along with the ability to withdraw money without penalty. However, the accounts that pay interest will typically require you to maintain a higher monthly minimum balance to either get the extra interest or avoid a monthly fee. You will want to have a checking account since this is where your money will be deposited into, and various bills will be paid from.

- **Savings Accounts** encourage you to save your money for a period of time. Some accounts pay interest on a statement cycle basis, others on an annual basis, and others after a specific period. These accounts are usually interest bearing, not typically used to pay bills or buy things, and are structured to encourage saving and therefore discourage withdrawals. Some savings accounts, often called "High Yield Savings," will offer you higher interest rates but lock your money down for a period of time and impose restrictions on your access to it. As a note, all bank deposits are considered safe because they are insured by the Federal Deposit Insurance Corporation (FDIC), which protects customer bank deposits in the event of a bank failure. The FDIC, the independent government agency that runs the program, was set up in 1933 to restore faith in the financial system during the Great Depression. After all, when you entrust your life's savings to a bank, you expect that money to be there when you need it. Typically, your deposits in a bank are insured up to $250,000.

- **Money Market Accounts (MMA)** or Money Market Deposit Accounts (MMDA) are a type of account that will pay you interest based on current interest rates in the money markets. Money market securities are short-term IOUs issued by governments, financial institutions, and large corporations. There is no formal money market, rather it is an informal network of banks, brokers, dealers, and financial institutions that are linked electronically. These are not money market investment funds, so the bank is still liable for your money. These accounts provide a more dynamic way to save money, are FDIC, provide a greater rate of interest on savings, and are a great way to start stashing away money you don't need to access for longer periods of time. MMAs have less restrictions than do savings accounts, both for you and what the bank is allowed to do with the money you have stashed there for their own investment portfolio. These accounts also usually have a higher minimum account balance requirement.

- **Certificate of Deposit (CD)** account usually allows you to earn more money than any of the accounts listed above. What is the catch? You have to commit to keeping your money in the CD for a certain amount of time. For example, you might use a six-month CD or an 18-month CD, which means you have to keep your funds locked up for six or 18 months. If you want to pull your money out early, you will have to pay a penalty.

- **Individual Retirement Accounts (IRAs)** are a great way for individuals to begin saving for retirement as they provide tax benefits. However, because of the tax benefits, there are specific rules for how much an individual can invest in a specific year and when an individual can take money out of an IRA (along with exceptions to these rules).

  - **Traditional IRA** lets individuals save for retirement and experience tax-deferred growth on their investments. This means that an individual can put money into an IRA, and they will not pay taxes until they withdraw the money on the amounts contributed, or the growth of that money. Each year that an individual contributes to an IRA, they may be able to deduct the contributions on their taxes. Because of the tax benefits, there are a few rules for opening, funding and withdrawing from an IRA. Only individuals who received taxable compensation and are younger than 70.5 years old can contribute to an IRA in a given year. The Internal Revenue Service (IRS) defines compensation to include salary, wages, commissions, self-employment income, alimony and combat pay. There are also limits to how much an individual can contribute in a year. For 2019, individuals can contribute up to $6,000 per year across all IRA accounts they own, unless the individual is at least 50 years old, in which case they can contribute up to $7,000. Contributions must be made by the following year's tax filing deadline. The deductibility of your contribution is based on your income and the numbers changed it each. Below is a chart that shows the contribution limits for 2019. Keep in mind that these numbers are different each year. Basically, if you're single and making below $64,000, you can fully deduct your IRA contribution. If you make over

$74,000, you cannot deduct any of it. If you make any amount in-between, you get a partial deduction which you will calculate at tax time.

Filing Status	Modified adjusted gross income (MAGI)	Deduction Limit
Single individuals	≤ $64,000	Full deduction up to the amount of your contribution limit
	> $64,000 but < $74,000	Partial deduction
	≥ $74,000	No deduction
Married (filing joint returns)	≤ $103,000	Full deduction up to the amount of your contribution limit
	> $103,000 but <$123,000	Partial deduction
	≥ $123,000	No deduction
Married (filing separately)	Not eligible	Full deduction up to the amount of your contribution limit
	< $10,000	Partial deduction
	≥ $10,000	No deduction

- Individuals cannot withdraw money without penalties or fines from an IRA unless they at least 59.5 years old. For early withdrawals there is a 10% additional tax penalty on the withdrawal. Once you reach 70.5 years old, there are required minimum distributions (RMDs), that require you to withdraw each year from your IRA. There are several exceptions to these rules, which are:

- Rollover: distributions from IRAs are exempt from early withdrawal penalties if rolled over into another eligible retirement account within 60 days.

- Distributions made to beneficiaries: IRA distributions made to beneficiaries of plans inherited after death are generally not subject to the early withdrawal penalty.

- Disability: disabled persons can take distributions from IRAs without being subject to the early withdrawal penalty. A disabled individual, for this purpose, is one that is "unable to engage in any substantial gainful activity by reason of any medically determinable physical or mental impairment which can be expected to result in death or be of long-continued and indefinite duration." The IRS requires proof of disability for this penalty exemption which includes substantiating documentation from a physician.

- Medical Expenses: distributions used to pay for medical expenses not reimbursed by health insurance that exceed 10% of your adjusted gross income are not subject to early withdrawal penalty.

- Health Insurance Premiums: withdrawals from IRAs used to pay health insurance premiums while unemployed are exempt from the 10% penalty if all the below requirements are met:

    - Unemployment compensation is received for at least 12 consecutive weeks.

    - The withdrawal is made the year unemployment compensation is received or the subsequent year.

41

- The withdrawal must be made prior to 60 days of employment at a new job.

- Higher Education Expenses: withdrawals from IRAs for qualified education expenses for you, your spouse, child, or grandchild are exempt from the early withdrawal penalty. The distribution cannot exceed the qualified higher education expenses incurred during the tax year. Qualified higher education expenses include tuition at a post-secondary school, room and board (if enrolled at least half-time), fees, books, supplies, and equipment required for enrollment or attendance.

- First-time home purchases: you may withdraw up to $10,000 from your IRA during your lifetime to pay qualified acquisition costs for a principal residence without being subject to the 10% penalty if you meet the IRS definition of a "first-time homebuyer," which means you have not owned a home in the two years preceding the purchase of your principal residence (if married, your spouse must also meet this requirement). This exception applies to the costs of purchasing your and/or your spouse's home or a home for your child, grandchild, parent, or grandparent if you or they qualify as a first-time homebuyer. The funds withdrawn from the IRA must be used to pay the acquisition costs by the 120th day after the distribution is received.

- **Roth IRAs** are like traditional IRAs but with one key difference: Roth IRAs allow an individual to invest money they've already paid taxes on and then withdraw the money later tax-free. Because of this, individuals cannot deduct contributions to a Roth

IRA on their taxes, and there are additional income require-ments for a Roth IRA. The absolute maximum amount an indi-vidual can contribute across all Roth IRAs that they own is the same as a traditional IRA but there are additional income re-strictions that can reduce the amount you can contribute or make you ineligible to contribute to a Roth IRA altogether. The table below shows the contribution limits based on filing status and Modified adjusted gross income (MAGI). Basically, if you're single and making below $122,000, you're fine. If you're making over $137,000, you cannot do a basic Roth IRA. However, you can do a backdoor Roth, which means you can contribute to a traditional IRA, without claiming a deduction for the contribution, and then convert your IRA contribution to your Roth IRA.

Filing Status	Modified adjusted gross income (MAGI)	Contribution Limit
	< $122,000	$6,000
Single individuals	≥ $122,000 but < $137,000	Partial contribution
	≥ $137,000	Not eligible
	< $193,000	$6,000
Married (filing joint returns)	≥ $193,000 but < $203,000	Partial contribution
	≥ $203,000	Not eligible
	Not eligible	$6,000
Married (filing separately)	< $10,000	Partial contribution
	≥ $10,000	Not eligible

- Like traditional IRAs, Roth IRAs have a 10% additional tax penalty for withdrawing money before you are 59.5 years old. Roth IRAs also require that the first contribution is made at least five years before you can withdraw money - so if you open and fund a Roth IRA when you are 57 years old, you cannot begin withdrawing money until you are 62. Certain exemptions apply. Unlike traditional IRAs, Roth IRAs do not have required minimum distributions. This is because you have already paid taxes on the monies that are in your Roth IRA. This means that you never pay taxes on the money in the Roth again, and more importantly, you never pay taxes on the growth of the assets within your Roth. The younger you are, the more it makes sense to do a Roth IRA since the long-term benefits of tax-free compound growth are massive.

- IRAs, whether traditional or Roth, provide great tax benefits. Contributions to a traditional IRA are tax deductible when you put them in and contributions to a Roth IRA are after tax, allowing your contributions to grow without taxes eating up any of the gains. Roth IRAs are also great for investors that expect their income tax to increase over time as an investor can contribute money at their current lower tax rate and withdraw the money later, tax-free. Even though the contribution limits mean that an IRA is unlikely to completely provide for you in retirement, the tax benefits make an IRA a great additional investment account in your portfolio.

- **Employer-Sponsored Plans:** I will not cover these in detail in this section, but many employers offer retirement investment accounts to their employees, such as 401(k)s or SIMPLE IRAs, and matching contributions to those plans for employees who contribute a certain amount per year. One of the best reasons to use an employer sponsored plan is the potential to receive a matching contribution from an employer - this is essentially free money. If an employer offers matching contributions, you should strongly consider enrolling in the plan and contributing at least the minimum to qualify for these matches. Employer sponsored plans also offer tax benefits similar to IRAs, allowing you to avoid taxes on gains that you may realize on your investments.

- **Taxable Brokerage Accounts** are one of the most basic types of investment accounts. These types of accounts can be opened individually or jointly. Unlike IRAs or employer sponsored plans, they offer no tax benefits, but they are free of the restrictions and rules that affect IRAs and employer sponsored plans. If you are contributing the maximum to your tax-benefited accounts, such as an employer's 401(k) or an IRA, and still have more to invest, then opening a taxable account is one way to continue investing. There are no limits on how much you can contribute to a taxable account. Unlike tax-benefited accounts, you can withdraw money at any time without penalty (though you may be subject to taxes on any gains you have to realize on these accounts) and there are no required withdrawals when you reach a certain age. Taxable brokerage accounts also offer more flexibility in the types of investments; employer sponsored plans may have limited investment choices and certain types of investments may be off limits in an IRA.

- Individual Taxable Brokerage Account- This is an investment account for one person to open, and it can hold a variety of financial assets, including stocks, funds, bonds, and almost anything in between. Any interest or dividends that you earn in a taxable account are subject to taxes in the year you receive them. Additionally, you may also be subject to taxes if you sell an investment. When you sell an investment for more than you bought it for, this is referred to as a capital gain, and when you sell at a loss, this is called a capital loss. If you sell an investment after holding it a year or less, your capital gain or loss is considered short-term; otherwise, it's considered long-term. Based on whether you sold an asset for a short-term or long-term capital gain, you will be subject to different taxes. Typically, it's better to hold investments for more than a year because the tax on long-term capital gains will be much lower than on short-term. If you sold any investments at a loss, you can also use your capital loss to reduce your total capital gain, offsetting some of the taxes. Unlike IRAs and employer sponsored plans, there are few to no eligibility requirements to open a taxable account (besides being at least 18 years old), no limits to how much an individual can contribute to a taxable account, and no restrictions on when an individual can withdraw money.

- Joint taxable brokerage accounts are similar to individual taxable accounts, except that a joint account is shared by two or more people. Most joint accounts are opened by spouses. However, if a joint account is opened by non-spouses, such as relatives or even friends, then there may be different tax implications, such as gift tax. If you're considering opening a joint account, make sure to clearly understand how taxes will be divided and paid and if there are any other taxes beyond capital gains, dividend, or interest taxes that you might incur.

How Do I Choose an Investment Account?

A good rule of thumb for picking an investment account is to start with accounts that offer matching contributions and/or tax benefits, if possible. If your employer offers a 401(k) or another plan, this is a great place to start, especially if you are new to investing. Employer sponsored plans typically offer fewer investment options than individual investment accounts, but this makes it easier for beginners to choose investments. Many even offer target date funds, which are an all-in-one investment consisting of a mix of stocks, bonds and other assets that are managed by the firm that runs the fund and requires little to no management on your part. Other plans may offer investment models, which require you to think about your risk tolerance before choosing a model, but then require no work on your part because the manager of the investments will handle the rest. Matching contributions from employers also make investing in employer sponsored plans a no-brainer.

If your employer does not offer a retirement plan, then consider opening an IRA account, whether traditional or Roth, to receive tax benefits on your investments. IRAs are great tools to begin saving for retirement and normally have more flexibility in the types of investments than employer sponsored plans. Roth IRAs are particularly good for investors who believe that their tax rate at retirement will be higher than it is currently. This is because a Roth IRA lets investors deposit money at their current lower tax rate and then withdraw the money later tax-free. Also, investors who are active or short-term traders would benefit from trading in a retirement account or employer sponsored plan to avoid large capital gains taxes.

If you find that you are reaching the maximum contribution limits for your employer sponsored plan and/or IRA and still have money to invest, then you should consider opening a taxable brokerage account. Investors should also consider opening a taxable account if they will be making withdrawals before age 59.5. For instance, if you need to save money for a down payment on a house or you plan on retiring early, then a taxable account may be a good alternative to a standard savings account. Because of the flexibility of taxable accounts, investors may use them to invest in assets that are not found or allowed in retirement or employer sponsored accounts, including collectibles or life insurance. Investors who want to invest in riskier, more speculative assets, such as options or penny stocks, may also choose to use a taxable account instead.

To open any investment account, other than an employer sponsored plan which must be provided by an employer, you can simply go online to any investment bank's website. I would recommend going with a low-cost provider such as Charles Schwab or Fidelity. Other options include trading platforms like E-trade or Scottrade, or the online investment arms of large banks, such as Merrill Lynch's Merrill Edge program. If you're not sure how to go about opening an investment account, then please talk to a qualified financial advisor so they can help you figure out the best type of account for you.

There are very few financial industry terms that are taught in school that are useful but there are some that you will need to constantly turn to throughout life that will help you navigate some important decisions so let's talk about one that will address most of what you're looking for.

Net Worth

Your Net Worth is the value of what you own minus what you owe. Or in fancy finance terms: assets minus liabilities.

Your assets (what you own) are things like:

- The value of your art collection

- The value of your shoe/purse/car collection

- The money you have in your bank accounts

- Anything you may have invested in anything else

- The "equity" in your home

  o The equity you have in your home is the amount of cash you would have in your pocket if you sold it. This means it's the value of your home today minus anything you still owe to the bank (or anyone else).

- Basically, anything you own that can be sold for money today.

Your liabilities (what you owe) are: Any debt you have of any kind which includes any amounts owed to banks, credit card companies, people, or loan issuers.

I want to be clear here: If you're renting an apartment or leasing a car, these are neither assets nor liabilities. There is no ownership occurring. These are simply expenses. They provide no value other than your ability to use them, but they are absolutely not an asset.

If your assets are greater than your liabilities, then you have a positive net worth. If your liabilities are greater than your assets, then you have a negative net worth.

Why is it important to know your Net Worth?

There are many reasons, but the two most important ones are rather simple:

1) You eventually want to have a very high positive net worth. This would mean that your assets are higher than your liabilities by a significant amount and therefore can presumably be liquidated over time to support your lifestyle.

2) You need to know what direction you're heading in so you can begin to prioritize your spending.

Once you know what your spending is, you know what your priorities are. Are you actively supporting Grubhub and Uber or are you working on accumulating assets? If it's the first of these two and you still have credit card debt, this may be an opportunity to make some changes. Take some time and figure out how you can start moving towards a positive net worth. Could you save more? Would it be prudent to realign your spending? Perhaps you can cancel cable for a few months and pay off some of your debt to get you a bit closer to your goals.

Chapter 4

Credit – Get it Right from the get-go

"Credit Card Interest Payments are the Dumbest

Money of All Time"

-Hill Harper

Let's talk about the one thing that seems to be a huge mystery for so many people. There is so much misinformation out there about credit, what helps to build it, what hurts it, and how you can fix it. There are entire books and businesses devoted to it. It's often exhausting just thinking about having to know all this and walk around thinking about it will make you want to never open a credit card or apply for a loan. However, we all live in a world where credit is incredibly important, so let's make it easy.

Credit measures the ability and trustworthiness of a customer to obtain goods or services before payment, based on the trust that payment will be made in the future[1]. Having "good credit" means you are trustworthy in the eyes of a lender and can likely pay back whatever amount they agree to lend to you. Having "bad" credit means that you are not trustworthy in this regard and will be unlikely to meet your obligations in the future. Whether you are considered trustworthy or not is based on several factors that all makeup a credit score which a lender or creditor uses

---

[1] https://en.oxforddictionaries.com/definition/credit

to determine if they are willing to lend you money. It also helps to determine the rate of interest that you will be charged in addition to the money you have borrowed.

There are five main factors that affect your credit score. For the purposes of this section, I am assuming you're an average consumer. An average consumer would be someone who does not own ten homes and is a multi-millionaire. We're talking about the common man here. Ranked from most important to least important, these factors are:

1. Payment History

2. Credit Usage

3. Length of Credit History

4. Credit Mix and Types

5. Recent Credit

Payment History

Having a long history of making on-time payments is best for your credit score, while missing or late payments would hurt it. For obvious reasons, the longer past-due you are, the greater the negative impact. For instance, a 30-day late payment would have a less damaging effect than a 60 or 90-day late payment. The amount of damage that is done to your credit for being late on payment would vary depending on the amount you owe.

Credit Usage

The amount you owe on installment loans, such as a personal loan, mortgage, auto loan, or student loan, is part of the equation. However, even more important is your current credit utilization rate. Your utilization rate is the ratio between the total balance you owe and your total credit limit on all your revolving accounts (credit cards and lines of credit). A lower utilization rate is better for your credit score. In very simple terms – this measures how much of your available credit you are using, and you should basically avoid maxing out your credit cards. In fact, to really keep your credit score in check, avoid using more than 30% of your credit card limit at any given time.

Keep in mind that you can pay your bill in full each month and still have a high utilization rate. Many people confuse their credit utilization rate with the balance they carry forward each month and the two are not the same. The calculation uses the balance that your credit card issuers report to the credit bureaus, often around the time they send you your monthly statement. You may have to make early payments throughout your billing cycle if you want to use a lot of credit and maintain a low utilization rate. Alternatively, you may want to ask if one of your credit card issuers would consider increasing your credit limit and you could just avoid using the new increased line.

Length of Credit History

There are multiple factors that play into this one:

- The age of your oldest account

- The age of your newest account

- The average age of your accounts

- Whether you have used an account recently

Opening new accounts, or taking out a new loan, could lower the average age of your accounts which may hurt your scores. It's also why I always tell people not to cancel their cards. Just leave them in a drawer somewhere never to be found again, and you will still be building the length of your credit history and increasing the average age of your accounts. Closing your oldest credit card could have a more dramatic impact on your credit score than you may imagine.

Credit Mix and Types

Having a history of different types of credit, like revolving credit card accounts and installment student loans, may help improve your credit score. Obviously, don't take out a loan and pay interest just to add to your credit mix, but if you have only ever had Installment loans (car loan or student loan, for instance), you may want to open a credit card and use it for minor expenses that you can afford to pay off in full each month.

Recent Credit/ Credit Inquiries

New credit inquiries: the number of times that a creditor runs your credit score to see if you're a viable candidate for a credit line - can stay on your credit report for up to two years. These are classified as either "soft" or "hard" inquiries.

Soft inquiries, for example, come from checking your own credit score and some loan or credit pre-qualifications, don't hurt your scores.

Hard inquiries, when a creditor checks your credit before making a lending decision, can hurt your scores even if you don't get approved for the credit card or loan. Multiple hard inquiries in a short period of time will impact your credit score. There is one exception to this: multiple inquiries for mortgages, auto loans, and student loans in a single 14-to-45-day period (depending on the loan and credit scoring model) may be treated as a single inquiry when calculating your score.

While you should be aware of the different factors that affect your credit, make sure you're keeping up with your own scores and verifying that the information appearing on your credit reports is accurate. This is the fastest way to figure out if your information or identity has been compromised in any way. There are several widely recognized credit reporting agencies including Transunion, Equifax, and Experian. You are entitled to check each of your own credit scores once per year for free. You don't have to check all three at the same time, in fact, I recommend that my clients check a different agency every four months on an ongoing basis. The correct (read: legitimate) site to check your credit is: www.annualcreditreport.com

Building credit can be tricky. If you don't have a credit history, it's hard to get a loan or even a credit card sometimes, and you need to have a responsible history of repayment in order to get almost anything – apartments included. Several tools can help you establish a credit history: secured credit cards, a credit-builder loan, a co-signed credit card or loan, or authorized user status on another person's credit card.

Credit cards are a great way to start building credit. Some important questions to ask any credit card issuer as it relates to credit cards:

1) What is the interest rate?

2) What day of the month is interest accrued onto the account?

3) What are all the fees and potential fees associated with this account?

4) What factors would result in an interest rate increase?

5) What factors are primarily considered for approval?

6) What is the "forgiveness" policy? In the event that life happens, and you miss a payment, you will want to know what the potential consequences are.

7) How often does the creditor report information to the credit reporting agencies and on which day of the month?

But what if you're already in trouble?

I don't like to be negative, but let's say that by the time you pick up this book, you have already managed to get yourself into some trouble with your credit. Let's say you have built up quite the credit card balance and you have no idea where to go from here. Below is my absolute best super general advice for getting out of debt.

Please know that I am not a credit expert, I don't work for a credit consolidation company, and this is most certainly not my main business. However, I've personally had to get out of credit card debt, I've helped literally dozens of peers get out of credit card debt, and hundreds of other people who have crossed my path throughout the years.

I would suggest that you avoid filing for bankruptcy at all costs. Bankruptcy destroys your financial future and there are so many professions that you would be precluded from if you have filed for bankruptcy in the past. Additionally, it will be terribly difficult for you to get an apartment, a new credit card, and some banks will not even hold your money if you have previously filed for bankruptcy. The entire world changes. Apparently, there is a rumor going around that if you file for bankruptcy, you get to just keep all the shit you purchased without any consequences. Let me be clear here: anyone who ever gave you a line of credit that you have not paid back is entitled to repossess anything you purchased from them if you default on that credit line. There is no such thing as a world that is free of consequences.

Additionally, credit consolidation can be extremely costly and can destroy your credit in the process. I have seen so many people hurt by their credit consolidation contracts that the whole thing makes me super weary. Don't get me wrong, I'm sure that credit consolidation helps thousands of people, but please read the terms of the agreement thoroughly. The way credit consolidation works is that someone takes over the debt you owe and gives you a new line of credit for the amount you owe. Let's say you owe $25,000 - you would now have a new loan for $25,000 with a new (hopefully lower) interest rate and new payment terms. You no longer have to make payments to your other creditors, only to the credit consolidator. While you go about your business paying off the new loan, the credit consolidation company is working to negotiate the amount you owe on your previous debt. They could do this in several ways, including repeated months of missed payments- until the creditors cave and are willing to take less money just to get something. In the meantime, on your credit report, you can be racking up constant late and/or missed payments, sending your credit score is down the drain. While it is true that recovering from credit consolidation takes less time and is generally less painful than recovering from bankruptcy. If you're anything like me, you would first be asking - is there anything else I could possibly do?

The answer is yes! And it's not too complex to boot!

Start by making a list of all your current credit cards along with their interest rates. Then arrange the list in order from highest interest rate to lowest interest rate. Next, call each of your credit card issuers from top to bottom (bonus points if you have more than one card with the same credit card issuer). You will then explain your situation - usually something like: it's getting really hard to make my payments on time and I'm considering filing for bankruptcy at this point because I'm so desperate, is there anything you can do for me? It may take talking to a few people in the company, but all credit card companies have what is called a "Hardship Payment Plan". These plans typically freeze that particular credit line for anywhere from one to five years and dramatically reduce your interest rate, with some offering zero interest for five years to get your balance paid off. You will not be able to use your card during this period, and it is up to the creditor if they choose to reopen the credit line for you once you're done making those payments. During the Hardship Payment Plan, your minimum payments would be reduced by about half, which will give you some wiggle room in your monthly income and expenses. This will allow you to start saving money, so that you can avoid getting yourself back or further into credit card debt at some point in the future. Best of all, these types of plans do not negatively impact your credit score if you stick to the plan and make all your payments on time.

This is super important. Learn from your mistakes and do better. If you are prone to getting yourself into credit card debt, then make sure you recognize that in yourself and get in the habit of using cash. One of my personal favorite things about these hardship plans is that they don't allow you to continue using the cards while you're on the plan which allows you to develop new habits in the process. Wherever you are in life, you have gotten there as a result of your habits and your decisions - plain and simple! Change your habits, change your life.

Student Loans

Since we're on the topic of credit, debt, and loans. I thought it would be an appropriate time to discuss student loans, and all the various types that are out there. Student loans are the big financial problem of our generation and many economists out there argue that it's likely the next economic bubble that is going to burst. What makes student loans even more difficult to handle is the fact that they cannot be escaped through bankruptcy. Even if you file for a bankruptcy, you will have to pay back your student loans. Fun stuff, I know.

If you're currently looking for a way to cover college expenses, you already have got a student loan in place and you're looking for the best way to pay it off, this section is for you.

In order to qualify for a Federal Student Loan, the first step is to fill out the Free Application for Federal Student Aid (FAFSA®). The FAFSA is the information gathering tool that the government uses to determine if you're a good candidate for federal aid, if you have the resources to pay for college on your own, or with the help of your parents. You will also want to apply for grants and scholarships, and line up work-study or part-time job opportunities. Your guidance counselor in your school should have a big book of the current year's available grants and scholarships to apply for. I personally recommend applying for every single one for which you meet the criteria. You never know, you could end up being the only one that applies for that scholarship and getting it by default. However, if your grants, scholarships, part-time work income, and personal assets are not enough to cover your college education, then you will need to take out some loans for your higher education expenses.

Federal Student Loans[2]

It's important to clarify what makes federal student loans unique when compared to private options:

- Interest rates are generally lower and always fixed.
- Credit checks and cosigners are mostly not required.
- Flexible payment plans and loan forgiveness programs may be available.
- Consolidating multiple federal loans can lower a monthly payment if the repayment plan is extended.
- Maximum borrowing amounts depend on grade level and dependency status, plus the cost of attendance.
- Loan servicers are chosen by the school or federal government, which also serves as the lender.

The federal loan program is robust and offers many different types of student loans. Though eligibility requirements vary, you could qualify for one or more of the following types of federal student loans:

1. Federal Perkins Loans (no longer available, but applicable for those who may already have them)

Before it expired in 2016, this school-based program was designed for undergraduate, graduate, and professional students who could demonstrate extreme financial need. In other words, students who come from low-income families or who are completely independent.

The advantage of taking out a Perkins Loan was that your school would pay the interest that accrued while you were enrolled. Not all schools offered Perkins Loans, and those that did might have had limited funds

---

[2] https://www.debt.org/students/types-of-loans/

to spread around. This sometimes resulted in needy students not receiving the maximum amount or not getting any support at all.

Interest rate: 5%

Maximum borrowed: $5,500 for undergraduates, $8,000 for graduates

Loan fee: not applicable

Term: 10 years

2. Direct Subsidized Federal Loans

Also known as Stafford loans, direct subsidized and unsubsidized loans have one significant difference: with subsidized debt, the Department of Education will cover the interest that accrues on your loans while you're enrolled at least half-time in college/university. For example, one year of interest on a $5,500 loan would be $206.80 for a Class of 2016 college freshman. If you qualify for a subsidized loan, the government will foot that bill for you.

Eligible undergraduate students must demonstrate a financial need to benefit from this. The schools to which you have been accepted will then detail the amount you can borrow in your college award letter.

Interest rate: 5.05% for undergraduates, 6.60% for postgraduates (for loans disbursed July 1, 2018, to July 1, 2019)

Maximum borrowed: $5,500 to $12,500 for undergraduates, $20,500 for graduates

Loan fee: 1.062% (for loans disbursed Oct. 1, 2018, and Sept. 30, 2019)

Term: 10 to 25 years

3. Direct Unsubsidized Federal Loans

Unlike subsidized federal loans, the unsubsidized version is also accessible to graduate and professional students, and awarding of the loan is not based on financial need or merit. In other words, almost everyone is eligible for this loan, if they are enrolled at least half-time in a college/university.

With unsubsidized loans, you're on the hook for interest that will accrue while you're enrolled, as well as during a grace period or if you defer your loan. What is more, the interest capitalizes when it goes unpaid, meaning that it will be added to the principal of the original loan amount, and therefore your monthly payments can increase significantly.

Interest rate: 5.05% for undergraduates, 6.60% for postgraduates (for loans disbursed July 1, 2018, to July 1, 2019)

Maximum borrowed: $5,500 to $12,500 for undergraduates, $20,500 for graduates

Loan fee: 1.062% (for loans disbursed Oct. 1, 2018, and Sept. 30, 2019)

Term: 10 to 25 years

4. Direct PLUS Loans

These loans, whether they are for students or parents, are unique in that they require the applicant to undergo a credit check. The Direct PLUS loan was specifically built for graduate and professional students who have had more time to improve their credit score (unlike undergraduates entering college, who might have never held a credit card).

To qualify for PLUS loans, a bad (or limited) credit history can be helped by a cosigner with excellent credit.

Direct PLUS loans also give their borrowers until six months after they finish or leave school to begin making payments.

Interest rate: 7.60% (for loans disbursed July 1, 2018, to July 1, 2019)

Maximum borrowed: The cost of attendance minus any other financial aid

Loan fee: 4.248% (for loans disbursed Oct. 1, 2018, and Sept. 30, 2019)

Term: 10 to 25 years

5. Parent PLUS Loans

This loan type is for biological, adoptive, and stepparents to support their dependent undergraduates. A key difference between Parent PLUS loans and other types of loans is that parents are expected to make payments while their children are in school, though they may request deferment during the loan application process.

The government does not offer a way for parents to transfer a PLUS loan to their children, but some private lenders do allow you to refinance a Parent PLUS Loan in a child's name.

Interest rate: 7.60% (for loans disbursed July 1, 2018, to July 1, 2019)

Maximum borrowed: The cost of attendance minus any other financial aid

Loan fee: 4.248% (for loans disbursed Oct. 1, 2018, and Sept. 30, 2019)

Term: 10 to 25 years

6. Direct Consolidation Loans

Consolidating any of the federal loan types previously mentioned allows graduates (or dropouts) to pool multiple loans into a single loan with a single loan servicer. This means you can make a single monthly payment, too.

That payment would also likely be lower than your past loans, as the repayment period can be extended up to 20 years.

Although consolidation is convenient, it's not right for everyone. It might give one borrower access to income-driven repayment options, but it might erase another's progress toward Public Service Loan Forgiveness.

Before deciding to consolidate, it's important to consider your own situation.

Interest rate: The weighted average of the interest rates on your existing loans

Loan fee: n/a

Terms: Up to 30 years

Private Student Loans

Even some private lenders will tell you to consider taking out federal loans before weighing their own products. This is because of the protections mentioned above that the government affords its borrowers.

Those same private lenders, however, will present their student loan options as customizable to your financial situation, while positioning the federal government's as one-size-fits-all.

The private loan details that can be personalized:

- Variable interest rates are offered, in addition to fixed rates.
- While cosigners are almost always required, a strong credit history can lower your interest rate.
- Repayment options, from deferment programs to in-school payments, can make your monthly bill more manageable.

When comparing private lenders to federal loan options, ensure that the little details important to you are not lost. For one borrower, this might be asking about prepayment penalties; for another, repayment protections might be critical.

1. In-school loans for students and parents

The beauty of in-school student loans in the private marketplace is that there are many to choose from. Whether you're a college freshman, a scholar seeking a doctoral degree, or are the parent of one - there is something for everyone. Sallie Mae, for example, offers 11 different education loans, from paying for the private kindergarten of your toddler to financing your study for the bar exam.

But with varying loan types come more choices. Take repayment as one example: College Ave, one of Sallie Mae's competitors, offers undergraduates four options while they are in school:

- Defer payments entirely
- $25 monthly payments
- Interest-only payments
- Full principal-and-interest payments

With this greater degree of decision-making, it's important to put private lenders to the test as you're shopping around. Don't rely on them to provide every bit of information you need to make a good choice.

2. Refinanced loans for graduates

Whereas the federal government's Direct Consolidation Loan allows borrowers to combine multiple federal loans into one, private lenders offer the option of refinancing federal and private loans into one new loan.

The key difference here is that consolidating federal loans does not directly save you money; it might actually cost you more, as the repayment term could lengthen.

Refinancing, however, could award you a lower interest rate and help you save on the total cost of your debt. A solid credit score and steady income can help you qualify for the lowest interest rates.

Private lenders are not shy about promoting their average customer's savings by refinancing. Although that number is important, consider whether you're the type of borrower who is likely to match that success. It's especially important to proceed with caution if you're refinancing federal loans and would lose their associated protections and forgiveness programs.

The Right Student Loan for You

Part of why private loan companies have enjoyed success in lending to students, graduates, and parents alike is that they are able to offer customized loans to creditworthy borrowers. Federal loans, on the other hand, were established to help cash-poor or credit-risky borrowers afford the rising costs of college.

Review all these student loan types before deciding what is best for you - and only you. Additionally, as you go through the college application and acceptance process, you may want to consider attending a college or University that gives you more aid if it's a close call between the schools.

Student Loan Repayment Plan Options

For Federal student loans there are several options for repaying your debt. Each option has its own benefits, and it is important to understand the details of each one so you can understand the best option for you. There are six repayment plan options in total, and they are:

Revised Pay As You Earn (REPAYE) is the newest of all the income driven repayment plans. It was created in December of 2015 as an extension of the previously existing Pay As You Earn (PAYE) plan, and was designed to remove some of the restrictions that were in the PAYE plan, as well as adding some benefits. The REPAYE plan caps your monthly payment at 10% of your discretionary income and provides loan forgiveness after 20 years of qualifying payments for undergraduate loans, and 25 years for graduate loans. There are currently three types of Federal loans that qualify: Federal Direct Loans, Stafford Loans, and Graduate Plus Loans.

A few benefits of REPAYE:

- Capped payment at 10% of discretionary income
- Payments qualify for Public Service Loan Forgiveness
- Complete loan forgiveness after 20-25 years
- Interest forgiveness for the first three years, and half of the accruing interest after year three.

There is one huge negative to the REPAYE plan which applies to married couples. Previous income driven plans would look at only the borrower's income if married but filing taxes separately from their spouse. Under the REPAYE plan, your spouse's income will be counted when calculating your REPAYE payment which can result in a much higher payment than other plans that do not have this clause.

The **Pay As You Earn (PAYE)** plan was passed into law on December 1, 2012 to try and improve upon the previously existing Income Based Repayment plan (IBR) . The PAYE plan caps your maximum payment at 10% of your discretionary income and the term for forgiveness is reduced from 25 years in the IBR to 20 years in PAYE.

There are a few restrictions to applying for PAYE. First, your payment in the PAYE plan must be less than what your standard ten-year payment would be. In addition to meeting the payment requirement, to qualify for the PAYE plan, you must also be a new borrower as of October 1, 2007 and must have received a disbursement of a Direct Loan on or after October 1, 2011.

Income-Based Repayment (IBR) plan is one of the older income driven repayment plans, which now has less benefits than the REPAYE and PAYE plans. It's still a great payment plan with strong benefits for the borrower, one of which is forgive ness on the first three years of any unpaid interest from when you enroll in the IBR plan for the subsidized portion of your loan.

For people with very low, or no income, this works out to be a form of "instant forgiveness" on their loans since their interest is not due. For example, someone with a loan amount of $50,000 and an interest rate of 6.8% would have about $11,000 of interest forgiven in their first three years from when their IBR begins. This assumes that you qualify for a zero payment. Another benefit of the IBR plan is that it typically offers the lowest payment for borrowers in financial hardship. The amount of your payment can never exceed 15% of your adjusted gross income over the poverty line for your family size. If you are married and file jointly, your spouse's student loan indebtedness can be taken into account and can further lower your payment. You may want to take advantage of an IBR plan if:

- You are having a financial hardship and would like some breathing room.
- You qualify for a payment of zero or payment of less than the monthly interest payment on the loan. This will allow for that interest to be forgiven on the first three years.

- You do not see a large increase in your income in the future, and see yourself always qualifying for a zero payment, in which case your student loan would be completely forgiven at the end of the term.

There is a formula for calculating the IBR payment and you will want to make sure to this site to make sure you get all the right information on your plan: https://www.studentdebtrelief.us/repayment-plans/income-based-repayment-plan/

Standard Repayment plans calculate the payment on your student loan like any normal loan payment – based on the size and term of the loan. Depending on your income and family size, the standard repayment plan can be a good option for you if:

- You want to pay off the loan as soon as possible and currently have less than 30 years left.

- You do not qualify for an IBR plan because of your higher income.

- Your loan amount is small enough where you can be paying a minimal amount over a short period rather than extending it for an additional X amount of years.

The standard repayment plan allows you to take care of your loans on time if you are making regular and full payments on them. You will pay less interest on a standard repayment plan than you will under the graduated plan. The term of your repayment plan depends on the size of the loan, and the chart below shows the maximum repayment period based on the amount of student debt you take on[3]:

TOTAL EDUCATION INDEBTEDNESS	REPAYMENT PERIOD MAY NOT EXCEED
Less than $7,500	10 Years
$7,500 – $9,999	12 Years
$10,000 – $19,999	15 Years
$20,000 – $39,999	20 Years
$40,000 – $59,999	25 Years
$60,000 or more	30 Years

Graduated Repayment plans are similar to standard repayment plans in calculation, but the major difference is that for the first few years under the graduated plan you are only paying interest on the loan. For this reason, your monthly payments under this plan will be lower than they would be under a standard repayment plan, in the beginning. You start off only paying interest on the loan and every two years, your payment increases. The term of the loan is the same as the standard and is based on your loan amount.

You may want to choose the graduated plan if:

- Your income is high enough where the income-based repayment programs do not make sense for you, or you don't qualify for them.

- You want to have a slightly lower payment right now, knowing that your payments will slowly increase every two years until the loan is paid off.

---

[3] https://www.studentdebtrelief.us/repayment-plans/

70

- You expect your current job to have normal and regular pay raises and expect to be able to pay the increase in the payment every couple years without it creating a hardship for you and your family.

One of the drawbacks of the graduated repayment plan is that the total amount you will pay back on the loan will be more than it would be with a standard repayment plan. This is because you are only paying off the interest for the first two years, and even into years three and four you may not be paying off the principal as fast as you would be in a normal amortization schedule. As such, you are left paying more through the life of the loan with the benefit being lower payments to start off.

Income Contingent Repayment plans use a couple of income-based factors to determine what your payment will be during your Student Loan Repayment. This plan calculates your payment two different ways, and then gives you the lower of the two payments. One calculation is your Adjusted Gross Income (AGI) over the poverty line for your family size, multiplied by 20% for an annual payment (divided by 12 for the monthly payment). This calculation does not take the loan size into account at all. The second calculation does use your loan value, an income factor determined by the federal government, and a constant multiplier also determined by the government. These are then used to calculate your payment for the second method.

You may benefit from an Income Contingent Repayment plan if:

- You are suffering a financial hardship and need relief.

- You do not see having a higher income in the future and would like to be eligible for student loan forgiveness. Under this repayment, it is not expected that at the end of the term the debt will be paid off, so loan forgiveness is likely.

Choosing a repayment plan for your student loans can seem like a daunting task. It is helpful to talk to your University's financial aid office and to discuss the payment plan with your loan servicer. You want to make sure that you evaluate the benefits of each plan and consider your unique financial situation. One of the considerations may be whether you are eligible for student loan forgiveness. It's also important to be aware that student loan forgiveness isn't free.

There are several ways to receive student loan forgiveness, including Public Service Loan Forgiveness, Teacher Student Loan Forgiveness, or through certain income-driven student loan repayment plans. Although student loan forgiveness might seem like a no brainer, there's one major consequence: taxes. Under current student loan repayment plans, if you have a remaining student loan balance at the end of your repayment period, then you may be required to pay ordinary income tax on any student loan amount forgiven. The result is a potentially massive one-time tax bill.

If you are a borrower with $50,000 of student loan debt that is forgiven, and a hypothetical 30% income tax rate (setting aside any potential tax deductions or credits), you would owe about $15,000 in federal income taxes. However, if you receive student loan forgiveness under the Public Service Loan Forgiveness program, then you are not taxed on any student loan amount that's forgiven.

Just remember that you may owe income taxes on the student loan amount forgiven. The less you pay each month under an income-driven repayment plan, the more interest is accruing on your loan. If you use an income-driven repayment plan to save money, you may lose those savings to taxes. Take all these factors into consideration before agreeing to a repayment plan.

Chapter 5

The 8th Wonder of the World

"Compound Interest is the Eighth Wonder of the World. He Who Understand it, Earns it, He Who Does not... Pays it"

-Albert Einstein

Albert Einstein called compound interest the "8th wonder of the world." I'm going to have to agree because this is such a powerful tool if you can understand and use it well, but also can be so destructive if you don't.

I often get questions like, "Why should I invest in anything? Why not just leave my money under my mattress?" Aside from the obvious – your house could catch on fire and your life savings would go up in smoke, the true answer is that you're missing out on the compounding that most investments offer. I know that I briefly covered this before, but repetition is the key to learning anything, and this is beyond important.

Let's start with: what is compounding?

In finance, compounding refers to the process in which an asset's earnings, from either capital gains or interest, are reinvested over time to generate additional growth. Basically, it's interest on interest. So instead of just your principal earning money (linear growth), your principal and the accumulated interest on your principal earns money.

Let's simplify further: suppose $10,000 is held in an account that pays 5% interest annually. After the first year, or compounding period, the total in the account has risen to $10,500, a simple reflection of $500 in interest being added to the $10,000 principal. In year two, the account realizes 5% growth on both the original principal and the $500 of first-year interest, resulting in a second-year gain of $525 and a balance of $11,025. That is right, you earned an extra $25 in the second year, the interest on the first year's interest. After 10 years, assuming no withdrawals and a steady 5% interest rate, the account would grow to $16,288.95.

Compound interest works on both assets and liabilities. While compounding boosts the value of an asset more rapidly, it can also increase the amount of money owed on a loan, as interest accumulates on the unpaid principal and previous interest charges. Compounding can also work against you if you have loans that carry very high interest rates, such as credit card debt. A credit card balance of $20,000 carried at an interest rate of 20% (compounded monthly) would result in total compound interest of $4,388 over one year or about $365 per month. You would literally be spending almost 25% more on whatever you're buying just by having a high interest vehicle that you use to cover some expenses. What is the point of buying things on sale if you're going to end up paying even more for them over time?

This is why paying yourself first is a fucking MUST! Nothing will destroy your financial plan as quickly as a high interest credit card that you don't pay off. Do not rely on credit in the event of emergencies. Build an emergency fund; it is such an empowering experience. I'm serious here, and there is a reason that I have written about this multiple times: you absolutely must pay yourself first, no matter what your cash flow situation looks like.

Random chart from the internet to illustrate all of this, below[4]:

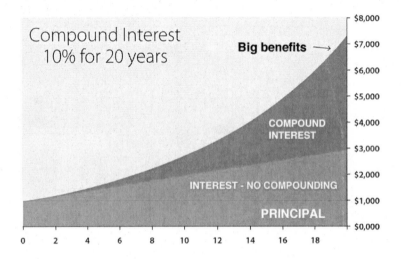

Do you know how wealthy people continuously create more wealth in their lives? It's compounding. When your investments are generating earnings that you are then reinvesting you are setting yourself on the path to true financial freedom, i.e. "fuck you money." There is no way to get to even your most basic goals without starting to build wealth, even tiny shitty little apartments typically require a security deposit and first and last month's rent. You will need to save. The further along you get in life, the more you will need to save, and it is significantly easier to start the habit when you first start earning money than it is to pick it up randomly in life.

Let's go back to my very first client, Lisa, who was a teacher her whole life, married to a principal and has retired with a massive nest egg that

---

[4] https://www.thecalculatorsite.com/finance/calculators/compoundinterestcalculator.php

very few people manage to accumulate. Do you think she did this simply by stashing money under her mattress on a regular basis? Of course not! She diligently saved each paycheck she got and invested it, earning compound interest along the way.

The biggest problem with the debt crisis of our generation is that we're paying huge amounts of interest and are not investing our assets in a way that helps us earn huge amounts of interest! If you're paying five or six % in interest on your student loans, don't you want your money earning something potentially similar? The biggest mistake you could make is keeping your savings in cash over the long term. You should expect to earn 6% to 7% in the stock market over any 10-year period. What are you earning on your cash? If it's anything like that last 10 years of cash savings, it's probably no more than 2% or so. Hmmm... something to think about, perhaps?

Chapter 9 of this dives deeper into the various investment vehicles and ways to get you to the point where you're actually taking advantage of these investment opportunities.

Chapter 6

You Just Got Hired… What is all this paperwork?

"Management cares about only one thing. Paper-work. They will forgive almost anything else - cost overruns, gross incompetence, criminal indictments - as long as the paperwork's filled out properly. And in on time."

— *Connie Willis*

Congratulations on getting the job!

Now that you have arrived, there is likely a stack of paperwork, either in print or on a web portal containing many super important decisions that you need to make within the first week, sometimes sooner, and you have never seen any of it.

Let's do a quick walk through of the forms you will typically see in your New Hire Package.

US Tax & Government Forms

Some of the forms you will receive are required by the Government, including a Form W-4 and a Form I-9. The W-4 form is an IRS form you complete to let your employer know how much money to withhold from your paycheck for taxes. A withholding tax is an income tax to be paid to the government by the payer of the income (your employer) rather than by the recipient of the income (you). The tax is thus withheld or deducted from the income that is due to the recipient. You will likely have a federal W-4, and if you work or live in a state that has state income taxes, you will likely also have to fill a state W-4 out as well. Accurately completing your W-4 can help you avoid having a big balance of taxes due at tax time, and at the same time can help prevent you from over-paying your taxes, putting more money into your own pocket during the year.

The W-4 is based on the idea of "allowances." The more allowances you claim, the less money your employer will withhold for taxes. You get one allowance for yourself, one for your spouse and one for each dependent that (your child or an adult who depends on you for more than 50% of their care) you report on your tax return. Claiming allowances can offset tax deductions you anticipate claiming, such as itemized deductions as well as for tax ramifications of claiming a particular filing status, such as "head of household" or if you're eligible to claim a tax credit for child care expenses. Your elections on the form also help you withhold extra money from your pay to cover taxes. If you work more than one job, have self-employment income or if your spouse earns income too, the personal allowance worksheet on Form W-4 will not incorporate this other income into your allowances, and too little might be withheld. This is because the additional income that you end up reporting on your tax return may put you in a higher tax bracket or may cause you to incur additional taxes associated with that income.

You can also use the W-4 to declare yourself exempt from withholding, meaning your employer will not reduce your salary for any federal or state income tax. You can claim an exemption from withholding if you did not have a tax liability in the prior year and you don't expect to have a tax liability in the current year. For example, if you are a single taxpayer who earns approximately $12,000 every year, then you will not owe federal income tax because of the personal exemption and standard deduction you can claim on your tax return. This effectively eliminates the possibility of owing tax on your $12,000 of earnings.

The W-4 form, otherwise known as Employee's Withholding Allowance Certificate, includes a series of worksheets you can use to calculate the appropriate number of allowances to claim. This includes a separate worksheet for taxpayers who have a working spouse or earn other types of income. Generally speaking, if this is your first and only job, and you are single, then you would claim 1 allowance - yourself! After calculating your allowances, you must provide some personal information and report your total allowances and additional withholding amounts on the actual form, and then give the certificate to your employer.

The IRS recommends that if you work more than one job, or if you and your spouse both work, that you claim all your allowances on the W-4 for the highest-paying job and claim zero allowances on the W-4 forms for all other jobs. It also suggests that taxpayers consider completing a new W-4 every time a major life event occurs, such as a marriage, the birth or adoption of a child, or a spouse getting or losing a job. These things can have a direct effect on the amount of tax you owe, so your W-4 should account for them.

The I-9 form, or officially known as the Employment Eligibility Verification, simply verifies your identity and employment authorization, it is mandated by the Immigration Reform and Control Act of 1986. New York state requires that every new employee be given a Notice and Acknowledgment of Wage Rate and Designated Payday, Hourly Rate Plus Overtime, which they are required to sign and return to their employer.

Consent and Disclosure for Background Checks/Drug Testing

If your new employer conducts background checks and/or drug testing, prior notice and consent from you is required. Such consent is typically obtained during the interview process but, if not, proper consents/disclosures are generally included in the hiring package.

Employee Handbook

Becoming familiar and acquainted with company policies and procedures is essential at the start of new employment. The handbook will address things such as the dress code policy, vacation policies, holiday schedule, human resource policies, and general information to help you make better decisions on how to show up for work.

Benefits and Insurance

If you're eligible for health insurance and other benefits, such as a 401(k) plan, a summary plan description will be included in the hiring package.

It is extremely fucking important for you to sign up for health insurance. If you land yourself in the hospital without health insurance, you can run up enough debt to pay for college 20 times over. Yes, health insurance is extremely difficult to understand but it is so important to your life- literally and financially.

You will encounter a whole alphabet soup of options while selecting health plans. The most common types are HMOs, PPOs, EPOs, or POS plans. The kind you choose will help you to determine your out-of-pocket costs and which doctors you can see.

While comparing plans, try and find a summary of benefits. A provider directory, which lists the doctors and clinics that participate in the plan's network, should also be available. Your workplace benefits administrator will have access to all of this. Your company's human resources (HR) department should be available to help you evaluate your options and to point you towards helpful information or resources.

Plan Type	Must stay in-network?	Specialist Referrals?	Best for you if:
HMO: Health Maintenance Organization	Yes, except for emergencies.	Yes	You want lower out-of-pocket costs and a primary doctor that coordinates your care for you.
PPO: Preferred Provider Organization	No, but in-network care is less expensive.	No	You want more provider options and no required referrals.
EPO: Exclusive Provider Organization	Yes, except for emergencies.	No	You want lower out-of-pocket costs but no required referrals.
POS: Point of Service Plan	No, but in-network care is less expensive; you need a referral to go out of network.	Yes	You want more provider options and a primary doctor that coordinates your care for you.

When comparing different plans, you will want to really examine your medical needs in depth. Look at the amount and type of treatment you have received in the past. Though it's impossible to predict every medical expense, being aware of trends can help you make an informed decision. If you choose a plan that requires referrals, such as an HMO or POS, you must see a primary care physician before scheduling a procedure or visiting with a specialist. Because of this requirement, many people prefer other plans. POS and HMO plans may be better if you don't mind your primary doctor choosing specialists for you. One benefit of this system is that there is less work on your end since your doctor's staff coordinates visits and handles medical records. If you do choose a

POS plan and go out of network, make sure to get the referral from your doctor ahead of time to reduce out-of-pocket costs. If you would rather choose your doctors, you might be happier with a PPO or EPO. An EPO may also help you lower costs as long as you find providers in network; this is more likely to be the case in a larger metro area. A PPO might be better if you live in a remote or rural area with limited access to doctors and care, as you may be forced to go out of network. Either way, there is no single right answer, so make sure you really look at what your ongoing care will cost you and plan to budget this into your fixed expenses. You certainly don't want to put yourself into a position where you're deciding between seeing a doctor and affording to eat a good meal!

Other types of insurance that may be offered:

Disability insurance covers you if you suffer a disability that does not allow you to perform the normal duties of your work. For instance, if you were a dentist and injured your wrist and became unable to move it, you may be unable to do most of the work that you currently do daily. This, disability insurance would protect you by paying you a portion of your regular salary, generally around 60%, until you are able to return to work. Disability insurance is significantly cheaper when offered through a group plan, like through an employer rather than if you were trying to purchase it on your own. You can also choose whether you would like to pay taxes on the cost of your disability insurance and receive your future disability benefits (if you ever needed them) tax free, or vice versa. I usually advise my clients to pay the taxes now so that their benefits are tax free in the future. This will also allow you to select a lower level of benefit – your net salary, instead of your gross salary.

There are two types of disability insurance: short and long-term. Short-term disability insurance helps workers replace lost income due to a temporary illness or injury that keeps them out of work for a limited time, this would include pregnancy, some injuries, and illnesses. You would use your short-term disability policy if you have run out of sick leave and are still unable to return to work for various medical reasons. Although some short-term disability policies can last up to two years. The typical policy lasts three to six months. Long-term disability insurance would kick in after you have run out of both sick time, and short-term disability. Long-term disability policies can last through people's age 65, 75, or even for life (if you have one of those magical unicorn lifetime long-term disability policies, don't ever let it go)! The purpose of these policies is to protect your income in the event something happens that prevents you from doing your normal daily duties.

Life Insurance pays a lump-sum benefit to anyone you choose if you die. It is very literally insurance on your life and should actually be called death insurance. Your employer likely offers some variation of a group term life insurance policy. They'll probably cover a basic amount, around $50,000 or so, and then you would have to pay for any additional benefit if you want it. Unlike with disability insurance, it generally makes much more sense to get an individual life insurance policy on your own rather than through your employer, and I generally do not recommend getting life insurance coverage through your employer. I'll go into further detail on life insurance in just a few chapters.

More importantly, in your benefits package will be information about your retirement plan and retirement savings options. This is where the power lies!

Employer-sponsored retirement savings plans are useful for both employees and employers and pack a huge punch of benefits - like having savings directly deducted from your paycheck, tax breaks, and in some cases, an employer matching your contributions. Say it with me - FREE MONEY!

Here are the seven most common types of employer-sponsored retirement plans.

1. 401(k) Plan

This is the most common employer-sponsored retirement plan today. It is primarily offered by medium and large for-profit businesses. It is a defined contribution plan funded primarily by the employee but often comes with at least a partial employer match. The employer will provide a menu of investment choices to the employee who chooses which investments in the 401(k) plan to put his or her funds into and will have complete control over the money upon reaching retirement. In addition, employee contributions are tax deductible in the year they are made. Investment earnings will accumulate on a tax-deferred basis. This means that anything you withdraw in retirement will be taxed at the ordinary income tax rate you pay at that time in your life. If you ever leave the job you're in you can, and should, take the money that you have accumulated in the plan, and the vested portion of the employer contributions (if any) and roll them into another retirement plan, like your own Individual Retirement Account (IRA), or your next employer's 401(k) plan. Any funds you withdraw but do not rollover into another retirement account are subject to ordinary income taxes and an early withdrawal penalty of 10%. There are annual contribution limits, which you can find online or get from or your workplace benefits administrator. There is also a catch-up contribution provision allowing those age 50-or-older to put more money away to help them get closer to their retirement goals.

As a note, IRAs, you will have a required minimum distribution upon reaching age 70.5. This means that you will absolutely have to begin withdrawing money from your 401(k) and pay the ordinary income tax on whatever it grows to by then.

2. Roth 401(K) Plan

Many employers today are also offering Roth 401(K) plans. These provide the same contributions as a regular 401(k) plan, but the benefits are slightly different. Contributions into a Roth 401(K) are not tax-deductible. However, distributions from the plan are completely tax free, as long as the employee is at least 59.5 years old and has been in the plan for at least five years. If distributions are taken earlier, the investment income portion of the withdrawals will be subject to ordinary income tax, as well as a 10% early withdrawal penalty. An employer can offer a partial match on a Roth 401(k); however, the employer contribution must be placed into a regular 401(k). The contribution limits are the same as they are with a regular 401(k) plan; however, the combination of contributions to both a 401(k) plan and a Roth 401(k) cannot exceed the annual contribution limit to a 401(k) plan. If distributions are taken early, they can be rolled over into only either a Roth IRA or another Roth 401(k) plan.

3. Defined Benefit Pensions Plans

These are often referred to as traditional retirement plans, and they used to be the most common type of employer-sponsored retirement plan, at least until the 1970s. Today they are super rare, and most have been replaced by defined contribution plans. In a defined benefit pension plan, the employee will receive a fixed monthly benefit at retirement and will not be responsible for making any contributions to the plan. All contributions will be supplied by the employer who will base the monthly benefit on income and years of service. All investment decisions will be made by the employer, not the employee, and since the plan is entirely administered by the employer, the employee will have no control over the funds upon reaching retirement age.

4. 403(b) Plan

The 403(b) plan is virtually identical to a 401(k) plan except that it's designed for nonprofit organizations. This includes public school systems, hospitals, home health service agencies, welfare service agencies, churches, and conventions and associations of churches.

The plans are funded primarily by employees and contributions are tax deductible when made. Employers can match contributions up to a certain percentage. Investment earnings accumulate on a tax-deferred basis, and contribution limits are identical to those of 401(k) plans.

5. 457 Plan

457 plans are basically 401(k) plans for state and local government employees. They work the same way as 401(k) plans and have identical contribution limits. There is one significant difference, however, between a 457 plan and a 401(k) plan. Should an employer offer both a 457 plan and a 401(k) plan, the employee can fully contribute to both plans, allowing for contributions that double the limit for a 401(k) plan.

6. SIMPLE Plan

SIMPLE stands for Savings Incentive Match Plan for Employees, which is an IRA plan offered by an employer. These plans are generally offered by smaller employers who do not offer more complex retirement plans.

The employee makes tax-deductible contributions to the plan, and an employer must make either matching contributions (up to 3% of the employee's salary) or nonelective contributions. Nonelectric contributions are funds employers choose to direct toward their eligible workers' employer-sponsored retirement plans regardless if employees make their own contributions. These contributions come directly from the employer and are not deducted from employees' salaries.

7. SEP Plan

A SEP is a Simplified Employee Pension plan that allows small businesses to have a simple method of administering a retirement plan for their employees. Like a SIMPLE plan, SEP plans are based on IRAs and are typically known as *SEP-IRA plans*. This has the same investment, distribution and rollover requirements as traditional IRAs; however, the contribution limits are much more generous.

Contributions are limited to the lesser of:

- 25% of annual compensation (though through a complicated formula, it works out to be 20% of your gross compensation), or

- The annual retirement plan contribution limit (the maximum any employee can contribute to all retirement plans combined)

Payroll Documents

Most, if not all, companies today use direct deposit. This means that your earnings will go directly into a bank account or multiple bank accounts of your choosing simply by completing the direct deposit enrollment form. This is much easier than trying to figure out how to cash your check and running to the bank every time there is a pay period. If it is easy enough to have your check go to multiple accounts, you will want to figure out how much you can save each pay period and have that amount go directly into your savings account.

Confidentiality and Non-Compete Agreements

Depending on the nature of the business you're joining, you may be asked to sign a confidentiality agreement, especially if you will have access to any trade or company-specific secrets. If applicable, you may also be asked to sign a non-compete agreement which is there to protect your employer in the event you end up being unhappy and decide to take your brilliant mind and work ethic somewhere else. Essentially, the agreement may limit you on where you can work, or if you can take clients with you. Make sure to read this carefully so that you know what your limitations are and can avoid potentially costly lawsuits.

Chapter 7

Income Taxes 101

"The Income Tax Has Made Liars out of More Americans than Golf"

-Will Rogers

There is nothing quite like the excitement and pride of receiving your very first paycheck. You worked hard for a solid month, and here is your hard-earned pay. But wait a second ... what is the story with this line that says "net pay?" That cannot be your actual salary, could it? What happened to all the money you made? By the time you get your paycheck, it's been cut up like a pizza, with several government agencies taking a piece of the pie. Exactly how much money is withheld from each check varies from person to person, company to company and state to state. However, almost every income earner has to pay federal income tax.

I'm going to try to explain taxes and our tax system in simply as possible. Although tax laws change all the time and differ from state to state, the general concepts should remain true for a long time to come.

The first income tax collected in the US dates back to 1863 and was a hefty 3% or 5% depending on what you made at the time. Income Tax collection was instituted and repealed several times over before it became a permanent part of our lives all the way back in 1913. The 16th Amendment reads, "The Congress shall have power to lay and collect taxes on incomes, from whatever source derived, without apportionment among the several States, and without regard to any census or enumeration." The 16th Amendment gave the government the power to levy taxes on people regardless of state population. The Underwood Tariff Act of 1913 included an income-tax section that initiated the progressive system we use today: Those who earned more than $3,000 ($4,000 for married couples) were subject to a 1% tax, which increased depending on income and topped out at 7%. I'm sure we all wish we could go back to the times of paying 7% in income taxes. During World War II, the federal government began withholding taxes, also known as the pay-as-you-earn taxation system. This gave the government the steady flow of money needed to finance the war effort.

While most Americans only think about taxes when April approaches, the tax collection process actually runs all year long. The process begins when you start a new job. You and your employer agree on your compensation - an hourly wage or an annual salary - which adds up to your gross or before tax income. As discussed previously, you then complete a W-4 to show how many allowances you have. After that, as required by law, your employer withholds a portion of your paycheck and sends it directly to a Federal Reserve Bank. This is how the federal government maintains a steady stream of income while also collecting interest on your tax dollars. Instead of paying taxes once a year in April, you really pay them throughout the year.

Some people love to get a big refund check when they file their tax return in April. But what that really means is that they paid too much income tax during the year. They could have put that money in the bank, invested it, or bought something useful with it rather than letting the government (or more accurately the IRS) borrow it. By adjusting the number of allowances on the W-4 form, you can decrease or increase the amount withheld from each paycheck. That way, there are no big checks or big bills in April. It's tax time and I'm sorry for all of us involved, which means everyone!

Filing income taxes in April is basically how you "settle up" with the IRS. Since you have been paying taxes all year long, in April all you are doing is determining if you paid the right amount. If you paid too much, you get a refund. If you paid too little, you're writing another check. Income tax forms like the 1040 are known for being as confusing as possible because they are based on a U.S. tax code that is more than 5,000 pages long. Here are the basic steps to completing a tax return:

1. Start by adding up your gross income (pre-tax income), which includes salary or wages earned from a job, investment income, interest income, pensions, annuities, and all other sources of income you may have. If you have a job, your employer will send you a W-2 form, either electronically or in the mail which shows how much you earned and how much income tax you have already paid through withholding.

2. Subtract any adjustments, such as alimony paid, deposits into retirement plans, self-employment or estimated taxes paid, interest that you paid on a student loan, and etc. The remainder is called adjusted gross income (AGI).

3. Once you know your AGI, you have two choices: Either subtract a standard deduction or subtract itemized deductions, whichever is greater. Itemized deductions include medical and dental expenses, charitable contributions, interest on home mortgages, and state and local taxes from the previous year. The standard deduction is currently $12,000 per tax-

filer. If you are married filing jointly then your standard deduction is $24,000. If your itemized deductions exceed your standard deduction, you would use your itemized deductions. The amount of these deductions is limited; read the instructions carefully.

4. Next, subtract your personal exemptions. Each year the IRS releases the number that they allow you to subtract for you, your spouse, and each dependent if your AGI is under a certain amount. Everything left over is called your taxable income.

5. This is where it gets a little complicated, because the United States uses a marginal or progressive tax rate system. The more you earn, the higher your tax rate. To determine exactly how much you owe, look up your taxable income on the IRS tax table, or for higher incomes the applicable Tax Rate schedule. The Tax table for 2019 Income taxes is below [5]:

Tax Bracket / Filing Status	Single	Married Filing Jointly or Qualifying Widow	Married Filing Separately	Head of Household
10%	$0 to $9,700	$0 to $19,400	$0 to $9,700	$0 to $13,850
12%	$9,701 to $39,475	$19,401 to $78,950	$9,701 to $39,475	$13,851 to $52,850
22%	$39,476 to $84,200	$78,951 to $168,400	$39,476 to $84,200	$52,851 to $84,200
24%	$84,201 to $160,725	$168,401 to $321,450	$84,201 to $160,725	$84,201 to $160,700
32%	$160,726 to $204,100	$321,451 to $408,200	$160,726 to $204,100	$160,701 to $204,100
35%	$204,101 to $510,300	$408,201 to $612,350	$204,101 to $306,175	$204,101 to $510,300
37%	$510,301 or more	$612,351 or more	$306,176 or more	$510,301 or more

[5] https://taxfoundation.org/2019-tax-brackets/

Find the number that matches your filing status: single, married filing jointly, married filing separately, head of household, or qualifying widow(er) with dependent child (same as "married filing jointly".) That number is your gross tax liability. There is one more chance from here to lower your tax bill.

6. From your gross tax liability, subtract any credits, as well as your withheld income taxes as shown on your W2. The Child Tax Credit is a big one. Other credits include the Earned Income Tax Credit for low-income working families, and the Child and Dependent Care Credit for childcare expenses.

7. The final number is your net tax. If it's a positive number, you owe money to the IRS. If it's negative, you're getting a refund.

As of the writing of this book, you must file your federal income tax return and pay any taxes owed by April 15, or at least file a request to extend the due date of your tax return, allowing you to file on or before October 15. Filing or paying late results in penalties and interest that accrue over time. If you are due a refund, the IRS either mails them out or electronically deposits them into your bank account within about two weeks of receiving a return.

If you are a freelancer, independent contractor or otherwise self-employed, no one is going to withhold income taxes each time you get paid by a client or customer. Instead, it's your responsibility to pay estimated taxes quarterly based on your taxable income the year before. Not only is it the law (you will have to pay a small penalty if you don't) but it allows you to avoid a big tax bill in April.

The reality is that most people don't file their own tax returns; they just hire an accountant or use simple software. I personally use TurboTax to do mine and my family's tax returns each year as it is inexpensive and easy to use.

Below is a not-so-brief list of everything you need to get organized with before you file your taxes:

Personal Information:

- Your Social Security Number

- Your Spouse's Social Security number (if married)

- Social Security Numbers for any dependents

- Your prior year's tax returns (if applicable)

Income Information:

Every dollar you earned in every which way you earned it. Bartering sheep for wood counts, really.

- W-2 Forms from all employers you, and your spouse if you're filing a joint return, worked for during the past tax year.

- 1099 Forms if you, and your spouse, completed contract work and earned more than $600 total.

- Investment income information

  - Interest Income

  - Dividend Income

  - Proceeds from the sale of bonds or stocks

  - Income from foreign investments

- Income from local and state tax refunds from the prior year

- Business income

    - Essentially accounting records for any business that you own

- Unemployment income

- Rental property income

- Social Security benefits

- Miscellaneous income

- Jury Duty income

- Lottery and Gambling Winnings

- Form 1099-MISC you may have received for prizes and awards

- Form 1099-MSA you may have received for distributions from medical savings accounts

Income Adjustments:

These can all help reduce how much you owe in taxes and increase your chance of receiving a tax refund

- Homebuyer tax credit

- Green energy credits

- IRA contributions

- Mortgage interest

- Student loan interest

- Medical Savings Account (MSA) contributions

- Self-employed health insurance

Credits & Deductions:

These will also help you lower the amount of tax you have to pay

- Education Costs

- Childcare costs

- Adoption costs

- Charitable contributions/donations

- Casualty and theft losses

- Qualified business expenses

- Medical expenses

Preparation for Direct Deposit:

(You know… in case you want your money being refunded to you faster)

- Your bank account number

- Your bank's routing number

Hopefully this makes it super easy to get organized. I honestly believe that gathering everything is like 85% of the effort in getting your taxes done. Cheers to hoping I can save the world from tax misery one chapter at a time!

As a note, you never want to skip out on paying your taxes, and every time you think about doing so, just remember that Al Capone, the world-renowned American Gangster during the prohibition era in Chicago, ended up going to prison not for his notorious gang related activity, but for two counts of tax evasion. The US government will forgive a lot, but they will not forgive the non-payment or under-payment of taxes and tax evasion is a criminal offense. I can make a very strong case as to why the IRS is the worst entity to ever be indebted to but just take my word for it and avoid it.

As a note, the best way to save money nearly instantaneously is to move to a state that does not have a state income tax. Seven U.S. states forgo individual income taxes as of 2018: Alaska, Florida, Nevada, South Dakota, Texas, Washington, and Wyoming. Residents of New Hampshire and Tennessee are also spared from handing over an extra chunk of their paycheck, though they do require you to pay taxes on dividends and income from investments.

Consider this: many people struggle to save ten % of their paycheck. If you're a resident of New York City, you're paying somewhere between six and seven % of your income from each paycheck to New York State, and another four % to New York City. There is your 10% Savings! Get up and move!

Chapter 8

So many insurances… so little time!

"Life insurance became popular only when insurance companies stopped emphasizing it as a good investment and sold it instead as a symbolic commitment by fathers to the future well-being of their families."

-James Surowiecki

When you enter the working world and start earning a living, it becomes apparent that many different types of people, with many different types of products and services, all want a nice healthy junk of the living you're making. This cannot be more evident in any other industry besides the insurance one. It seems there is a type of insurance available to protect you from absolutely everything.

The most common types of insurance that you should consider purchasing are: Life Insurance, Disability Insurance, and Long-term Care Insurance. Each one of these has multiple types and has a wide range of costs associated with it.

Life Insurance.

So many ways, so many different types. So much... fuss.

Honestly, every life insurance agent will find a way to solve any problem you have by selling you life insurance. As always, the more you know, the less likely you are to get ripped off so let's break it down!

Life Insurance – Insurance you purchase on your life (or someone else's) that is paid out upon the death of the insured. Theoretically, you would only be purchasing this out of a financial need. So, for example, if you don't have children, and literally NO ONE will suffer financially if you are gone, you probably don't need life insurance. Burials may cost too much these days, but a $1 million whole life policy is NOT necessary to account for a burial and funeral... I promise.

Types of Life Insurance:

- Term Life Insurance

    - Life Insurance for a specific time period, or term, i.e. 10 years, 20 years, 30 years, etc.

    - This is the cheapest type of life insurance.

    - MOST people will only ever NEED a Term policy.

    - No bells and whistles, it is literally the simplest type.

    - Does not build cash value.

    - Once you stop paying, or when you reach the end of the term, it goes away and is worth nothing.

    - This is like renting a life insurance policy. You only have it for the period of time that you need it. Once you no longer need it, you no longer have it.

- Whole Life Insurance

    - Life Insurance for your WHOLE LIFE - however long that is.

- Generally, has a pretty high premium since it accounts for the projected cost of insurance when you are 99 years old (which is high).

- Builds cash value.

  - A portion of your premiums are paid into the investment account, or the cash value, and this money grows with interest over time. If you want to cash inf your life insurance early and surrender your coverage to the insurer, you will receive the policy's cash value minus fees.

- A portion of your annual premium goes towards paying the cost of insurance/expenses and a portion goes towards cash value. Usually these policies have a minimum guaranteed "rate of return" built into them. The cash value may be used in the future to reduce your premiums.

- If you under pay your premiums, you risk that the policy lapses, or blows up, when you are older, and you will have paid in for nothing, and may land yourself a nice tax bill for any interest earned in the policy while you had it.

- If you already have a whole life policy, PLEASE make sure to ask the company through which you purchased it for an in-force illustration at least once per year. This will show you the projected life span of the policy and will also show you the performance of the policy. You can compare the illustration you get each year, to the original illustration issued with the policy to make sure it's performing the way it's supposed to.

- Universal Life Insurance
  - Like a term life policy that lasts for your whole life.
  - Generally, more expensive than term life but cheaper than Whole Life.
  - You basically get to pick how much premium you want to pay into the policy. There is a "suggested" premium amount which you could pay every year and theoretically keep the policy in force for life. Anything you pay over that amount is considered excess premium payments. The total excess of premium that you pay over the current cost of insurance is credited towards the cash value in the policy. The cash value is credited each month with interest, and the policy is debited each month by a cost of insurance (COI) charge, as well as any other policy charges and fees drawn from the cash value, even if no premium payment is made that month.
  - Usually the cash value works on an arch – the value will build up while you're young and then dramatically start to tumble as the cost of insurance increases in older ages. Reminder that the cost of insurance is always increasing as you age.
  - These policies need to be constantly evaluated for risk of lapsing. The cost of insurance can be changed at any time by the insurance company and you never want to completely run out of value in the policy. Like with Whole Life, if you already have a Universal Life policy, please ensure

that you request an in-force illustration on the policy each year.

- Variable Life Insurance

    - Variable life insurance is a permanent life insurance policy with an investment component. The policy has a cash value account, which is invested in several sub-accounts available in the policy. A sub-account acts like a mutual fund – charges expenses/fees, and *hopefully* provides a return.

    - The investment return and principal value of variable sub-accounts will fluctuate. Your cash value, and perhaps the death benefit will be determined by the performance of the chosen sub-accounts. Variable universal life insurance policies typically include mortality and expense risk charges, administrative fees, and fund expense charges.

- Survivorship Life Insurance

    - Insures two people, usually a married couple, and generally benefits their heirs or survivors.

    - Is cheaper than other cash value policies because it is based on two lives.

    - Is cheaper than buying two separate policies.

    - May help with estate tax burdens.

I'm generally not in favor of purchasing whole life and universal or variable policies so to make things a bit fairer, here are some benefits of cash value policies:

- You can borrow against them.

- You don't have to wait to die to use them - you can create an income stream from the cash value. Please note that this would create a taxable event in most life insurance policies.

- You can always increase your own benefit by pouring more money into the policy.

- You can also decrease your benefit by reducing how much you put into the policy.

- Lifelong protection.

- Cashflows grow income tax free.

- Death Benefits are generally paid to beneficiaries free from income tax.

- Provide protection against creditors in many states.

- Are not counted in assets for college planning purposes.

The biggest issue with the life insurance industry today is that life insurance is something that people are continuously sold instead of it being about meeting the needs of the individual. There are now life insurance policies that purport to solve almost any financial problem you have; however, they are likely not the best tool for solving every problem.

Life insurance should only be purchased if you have an insurable need. For instance, almost every single person or couple with a young child should absolutely have life insurance, unless you have so much in assets that you can fully support the life of the child if something happened to you. Additionally, you likely don't need the same dollar amount of coverage when your children are sixteen compared to when your children are five or six. The cost of care you provide for your child goes down over time. At the same time, hopefully, your savings and the ability you have to self-insure goes up over time. I usually tell my clients that, if you have the liquidity to retire you don't need life insurance. That also means that, you don't need permanent life insurance.

Once you have decided that you absolutely need to have life insurance, the next most important thing to figure out is how much life insurance you actually need. A good way to do this is to take your large expenses and then add in the present value of a future income stream. If you're lost in all this, don't worry, I'll explain:

I'm going to use my clients, Annie and Stan, as the example for this since they recently purchased some life Insurance. Annie is 31 years old, and she's married to Stan who is 33 years old. They have one three-year-old daughter and a son on the way. Annie currently earns $150,000 per year working in advertising. Stan has his own accounting practice and makes about $200,000 per year. They currently own a beautiful home out in Long Island which they have about a $700,000 mortgage left on. The current cost of putting a child through college, counting tuition at a private four-year university and room and board is just about $200,000. That means that at minimum, they would need $1,100,000 in life insurance coverage for the next 25 years or so to cover the mortgage and the cost of college for each of their kids. However, we did not take their general cost of living into account. Let's say that they spend about $180,000 per year, net of taxes. That means that on top of covering their major expenses, they'd want to be able to replace the income that each person is contributing to the household. Clearly, neither Annie nor Stan alone would be able to support $180,000 in annual expenses on their own. They need each other's income streams to support their lifestyle. Annie would need to cover slightly more of that $180,000 than Stan would. The total present value of 25 years of receiving $180,000, adjusted for inflation at 2.5% is just over $3,300,000. In the event that something happened to both of them today, and they wanted to provide their children with the same lifestyle they are used to living, they would need to leave behind $3,300,000 plus $1,100,00 to cover the major expenses.

Since Annie earns less than Stan, he would need to leave behind a large chunk of this if something were to happen to him. As such, in this instance, I would recommend a total of $3,100,000 of insurance on Stan's life, and a total of $2,400,000 million of life insurance on Annie's life. However, ten years from now, I would recommend significantly less life insurance. The kids will be ten and seven years old which costs slight less to care for and oversee compared to a three old and a baby. More importantly, Annie and Stan would have earned income and saved money for ten years of their life.

Ten years from now, they will have paid down a large chunk of their mortgage, maybe even a third of it. They would have saved money along the way, and they would be spending less on child care. Note that they would still have the prospect of paying for college for their kids as a major expense item. As such, what they really need is multiple insurance policies that create a laddered effect. We ended up structuring it like this:

Annie:

10-year term policy for $1,000,000

20-year term policy for $500,000

30-year term policy for $1,000,000

This means that Annie has $2.5 million in life insurance coverage for the next 10 years, then $1.5 million of insurance for the 10 years after that, and $1 million of insurance for the last 10 years. Annie made a decision to cover them for a full 30 years because she wanted to leave her kids a large sum of money if something were to happen to her when they were still in their 20's.

Stan

10-year term policy for $1,000,000

20-year term policy for $1,000,000

30-year term policy for $1,000,000

This means that Stan has $3 million in life insurance coverage for the next 10 years, then $2 million of insurance for the following 10 years after, and $1 million of insurance for the last 10 years.

If something happened to both at the same time, their kids would receive a total of $5.5 million today and for the next 10 years, $3.5 million for the 10 years after that, and $2 million for the last 10 years.

I think we can all agree that this is a financially sound structure for this family. The great benefit of using a laddered term insurance policy is that the cost of term insurance is significantly lower than it would be to cover a large lump sum over a 30-year period, and the cost goes down every 10 years! This means that the family could save more money on their own as the cost of their insurance goes down over time.

This is just an example of a creative way to use life insurance to cover insurable needs. A typical insurance agent may offer a $3 million 30-year term policy, but that would just create an additional expense for the client that's unnecessary. There are so many extremely cost-effective ways to use life insurance to solve your issues. Unfortunately, permanent insurance usually isn't one of them. As a basis for comparison, a $1 million 30-year term policy issued to a healthy 31-year woman would cost about $850 in annual premiums. The same $1 million Whole Life policy would cost about $12,000 in annual premium. Whole life insurance tends to cost ten to twelve times as much as term insurance. Yes, there is a savings aspect to it, but there is nothing that the insurance company is doing, in terms of savings, that you cannot do on your own. So you end up paying high administration costs and other fees just for the "benefit" of having a forced savings account.

Disability Insurance

Disability insurance pays part of your income if you cannot work because of an illness or injury. You can get coverage through an employer or buy it from an insurer.

Your most valuable asset isn't your house, car, or retirement account. It's your ability to make a living. The chance of missing months or years of work because of an injury or illness may seem remote, especially if you're young and healthy and you work at a desk. However, more than one in four 20-year-olds will experience a disability for 90 days or more before they reach 67, according to the Social Security Administration[6].

One reason people shrug off the risk is they think about worst-case scenarios, such as spinal cord injuries leading to quadriplegia or horrific accidents that result in amputation which could be covered by Medicaid. However, back injuries, cancer, heart attacks, severe diabetes, and other illnesses result in most disability claims.

There are two main types of disability insurance: short-term and long-term coverage. Both replace a portion of your monthly base salary up to a cap, such as $10,000, during disability. Some long-term policies pay for additional services, such as training to return to the workforce.

---

[6] https://www.ssa.gov/news/press/factsheets/basicfact-alt.pdf

108

Disability policies vary in how they define "disabled." Some policies pay out only if you cannot work any job for which you're qualified. Others pay out if you cannot perform a job in your occupation. Some policies cover partial disability, which means they pay a portion of the benefit if you can work part time. Others pay only if you cannot work at all.

Short-term disability insurance	Long-term disability insurance
Typically replaces 60% to 70% of base salary	Typically replaces 40% to 60% of base salary
Pays out for a few months to one year, depending on the policy	Benefits end when the disability ends. If the disability continues, benefits end after a certain number of years or at retirement age.
May have a short waiting period, such as two weeks, after you become disabled and before benefits are paid	A common waiting period is 90 days after disability before benefits are paid

There are multiple ways to get coverage:

- Sign up for employer-sponsored coverage at work. Most employers that offer disability insurance pay some or all the cost of premiums. Five states provide or require employers to provide short-term disability benefits: California, Hawaii, New Jersey, New York and Rhode Island.

- Buy disability insurance through the workplace. Some employers don't pay for disability coverage but do offer it as a voluntary benefit. This lets employees buy coverage through the employer's insurance broker at a group rate. You always want to try and get a group rate since individual disability insurance plans are much more expensive.

- Buy disability insurance through a professional association. Many professional groups offer members coverage at group rates.

- Buy an individual disability insurance plan. You can get it from an insurance broker or directly from an insurance company. Big sellers of

109

individual disability insurance include Guardian, MassMutual, Northwestern Mutual, Prudential, and Principal. Most individual disability policies sold are for long-term coverage, although some companies also offer short-term policies.

Buying your own disability policy:

Consider buying a policy if you don't have any or enough disability coverage at work or are self-employed. Employer-sponsored disability insurance usually pays only a portion of your base salary, up to a cap. It's a good idea to supplement that coverage if your salary far exceeds the cap or you depend on bonuses or commissions. An insurer will consider other sources of disability insurance to determine how much coverage you can buy. Generally, you cannot replace more than 75% of your income from all the coverage combined. You may not need to cover 75% of your income. Many individuals can choose 50% to 60% coverage which may be enough for you.

Buying your own policy lets you:

- Customize the coverage with extra features, such as annual cost-of-living adjustments.

- Choose the insurance company with the best offerings.

- Keep the coverage when you change jobs. Employer-paid coverage ends when you leave the company. (You might be able to take the coverage if you pay the full premium for disability insurance offered through the workplace.)

- Control the disability insurance. The coverage stays intact as long as you pay for it. But employer-sponsored coverage will end if the employer decides to stop providing disability benefits.

- Collect benefits tax-free if you become disabled. If the employer pays for the coverage, you must pay taxes on the benefits.

Many disability policies you purchase on your own come with fun bells and whistles. Make sure you seek the advice of a competent financial planner or disability insurance representative to figure out what is right for you.

The following programs also offer financial help in case of a disability, but they have limitations:

- Social Security pays disability benefits, but it's difficult and time-consuming to qualify, and the payments are low. The average monthly disability benefit in 2019 is $1,234.[7]

- State disability programs are offered in California, Hawaii, New Jersey, New York and Rhode Island. They provide short-term disability coverage, in most cases for up to six months.[8]

- Workers' compensation insurance replaces a portion of income if you're disabled because of a work-related injury. All states require employers to have workers compensation coverage for their employees. Most long-term disabilities are not the result of work-related injuries, however.

Long-term Care Insurance

A long-term care insurance policy helps cover the costs of care when you have a chronic medical condition, a disability or a disorder such as Alzheimer's disease. Most policies will reimburse you for care provided

---

[7] https://www.disabilitysecrets.com/how-much-in-ssd.html
[8] https://eligibility.com/social-security-disability

in a variety of places, such as your home, a nursing home, an assisted living facility, or an adult day care center.

Long-term care insurance is expensive. Not everyone can afford it, and some wealthy individuals don't need it. But considering long-term care costs are an important part of any long-range financial plan, especially when you're in your 50s or older. Waiting until you need care to buy coverage is not an option. You will not qualify for long-term care insurance if you already have a debilitating condition. Most people with long-term care insurance buy it in their mid-50s to mid-60s. Whether long-term care insurance is the right choice depends on your situation and preferences. Consider seeking the help of an advisor if you, or someone you know, is in a place in their lives where they need to start considering long-term care. According the U.S. Department of Health and Human Services, of those aged 65-and older, 70% will use some form of long-term care[9].

I will not go into further depth on long-term care insurance in this book but please do some research and figure out if this is something you or a loved one needs. Long-term care costs are extremely high and can deplete a legacy in just a few years.

[9] https://longtermcare.acl.gov/the-basics/how-much-care-will-you-need.html

Chapter 9

Investments

"One of the funny things about the stock market is that every time one-person buys, another sells, and both think they are astute."
-William Feather

I think that it's time for us to finally touch upon investments. There are so many different investment types and vehicles out there. Keeping in line with the original mission of this book, I want to give you a holistic overview and just enough detail for you to feel empowered. The average investor, especially in the beginning of his or her investing timeline tends to have some combination of the four basic types of investments. Most people have heard all of he below terms before, probably thousands of times, and yet I constantly come across people who don't know what they are. So here we go:

Stocks (or equities)

A stock is a share of ownership that is issued by a company to raise funds. Stock represents a claim on the company's earnings (and losses). Owning one share of a company's stock makes you a "share-holder". Many people confuse owning shares of a company with owning the assets of the company; this is incorrect. The chairs and tables at the corporate office still belong to the corporation, not to the shareholders. Owning stock usually gives you the right to vote in shareholder meet-ings, receive dividends (which are a distribution of company's profits) if

113

and when they are distributed, and it gives you the right to sell your share or shares to somebody else.

If you own the majority of shares in a company, your voting power may be such that you can indirectly control the direction of a company by appointing its board of directors. This is not so relevant to the average person but very relevant when a company buys another company.

Stocks are also issued by companies to raise capital in order to grow the business. By buying shares of the company, you're essentially betting that you will make money because you think the company will grow, or profits will increase. Just keep in mind, companies don't always grow, and very often they go bust - so you risk losing the money you invested in the stock.

Bonds

Bonds are fundamentally different from stocks. Bonds are a loan that purchasers of bonds are giving to a company, government, or municipality. Bondholders are creditors to the issuer of the loan and are entitled to interest as well as repayment of principal. Creditors are given legal priority over other stockholders in the event of a bankruptcy and will recoup their money first if a company is forced to sell assets in order to repay them. This inherently makes them significantly safer and less risky than stocks. Shareholders are last in line and usually receive nothing, or a few pennies on the dollar, in the event of bankruptcy.

On the flip side, bondholders are only entitled to receive the return given by the interest rate agreed upon by the bond, while shareholders can get great returns generated by increasing profits, theoretically to infinity.

Bonds, unlike stocks, are also subject to interest rate risk. Interest rate risk is the risk that changes in interest rates (in the U.S. or other world markets) may reduce or increase the market value of a bond you hold.

Interest rate risk, categorized as market risk, increases the longer you hold a bond. When interest rates fall, bond prices rise, and when interest rates rise, bond prices fall. Let's use an example to demonstrate this:

Say you bought a 10-year, $1,000 bond today at a coupon (interest) rate of 4 %, and interest rates rise to 6 %. If you need to sell your 4 % bond prior to maturity, then you must compete with newer bonds carrying higher coupon rates. These higher coupon rate bonds decrease the appetite for older bonds that pay lower interest (i.e.: your 4% bond). This decreased demand lowers the price of older bonds in the secondary market, which would translate into you receiving a lower price for your bond if you need to sell it.

Rising interest rates also make new bonds more attractive because they earn a higher coupon rate. This results in what is known as opportunity risk – the risk that a better opportunity will come around that you may be unable to act upon. The longer the term of your bond, the greater the chance that a more attractive investment opportunity will become available, or that any number of other factors may occur that negatively impact your investment. This is also referred to as holding-period risk – the risk that not only a better opportunity might be missed, but that something may happen during the time you hold a bond to negatively affect your investment. The ability to avoid these risks is why short-term bonds are said to be a safer investment than longer-term bonds.

Bonus point: many municipal and government issued bonds are tax advantaged. For instance, a New York City (NYC) resident owning a NYC school bond will not pay any taxes on the interest income received from the bond. Therefore, a 4.5% NYC bond will net you more income than a 5% corporate bond.

Mutual Funds

A Mutual Fund is an investment vehicle made up of a pool of monies collected from many investors for the purpose of investing in securities, such as stocks, bonds, money market instruments, and other assets. Mutual funds are operated by professional money managers, who allocate the fund's investments and attempt to produce growth in the portfolio and/or income for the fund's investors. A Mutual Fund will usually have a stated investment objective and as such, the investments are made to align with the stated objective.

When thinking about how these operate, just remember the word Mutual. All the expenses are shared, all the costs are shared, all the gains are shared and, of course, all the losses are shared. The amount of each that a shareholder of the fund will experience is directly proportional to the amount of the fund that the shareholder owns. When you buy a share of a mutual fund, you are actually buying the performance of its portfolio. The pooling of assets in a mutual fund can provide greater diversification than smaller investors would otherwise be able to access.

A mutual fund is both an investment and an actual company. This is strange, but is actually no different than how a share of AAPL is a representation of Apple, Inc. When an investor buys Apple stock, they are buying part ownership of the company and its assets. Similarly, a mutual fund investor is buying part ownership of the mutual fund company and its investment assets. The difference is that Apple is in the business of making computers and smartphones, while a mutual fund company is in the business of making investments. Mutual funds are typically bought and sold once per day based on the closing prices of the markets where its holdings trade.

Exchange Traded Funds (ETF)

An ETF is a marketable security that tracks an index, a commodity, bonds, or a basket of assets like an index fund. Unlike Mutual Funds, an ETF trades like common stock on a stock exchange. ETFs experience price changes through the day as they are bought and sold and typically have higher daily liquidity and lower fees than mutual fund shares.

An ETF owns the underlying assets (shares of stock, bonds, oil futures, gold bars, foreign currency, etc.) and divides ownership of those assets into shares. Shareholders do not directly own or have any direct claim to the underlying investments in the fund, but they do own these assets indirectly. ETF shareholders are entitled to a proportion of the profits, such as earned interest or dividends paid, and they may get a residual value in case the fund is liquidated. The ownership of the fund can be easily bought, sold or transferred in much the same way as shares of stock.

By owning an ETF, investors get the diversification of an index fund as well as the ability to sell short, buy on margin, and purchase as little as one share (there are no minimum deposit requirements). The expense ratios tend to be significantly lower than those of most mutual funds.

General Investment Guidance

There are literally hundreds of different types of investments and investment vehicles out there but these four are usually the core of any diversified portfolio and the core of most newspaper articles out there. So now when someone talks about Mutual Funds in Investment News, you know a little more about what they are referring to and why it matters.

When should you start investing? Now. Invest now, not tomorrow.

One of the simplest ways to start investing is to contribute to your employer's 401(k) plan, a tax advantaged retirement savings account, or to other retirement savings accounts, such as a Roth IRA or traditional IRA. The biggest gift you can give yourself is to start investing as early as possible.

Take someone, let's call him Mike, who starts investing at age 19 and invests for eight years until he's 27. He invests a total of $28,800, or $300 per month, and then just leaves it there—does not add another penny. He'll have nearly 2 million when he retires at 65 if the market continues to compound at the historical average of 10% annually. His friend, David, on the other hand, does not start till he's 28 and he invests $300 a month, he'll have invested $140,000 by the time he retires at 65. But his compounding returns will end up at almost $300,000 less than Mike's. You will notice that in this example, David ends up saving more and for longer than Mike, but still ends up with less money [10]. The magic of compounding happens when you start investing as early as possible.

Now, every time I talk to people about investing, they always ask: what stock do I buy?

The answer is: don't buy stocks, buy index funds.

I'm going to take the Warren Buffett and Tony Robbins approach here and explain to you why buying index funds is absolutely the best way to get started.

Index funds hold every stock in an index such as the S&P 500, including big-name companies such as Apple, Microsoft and Google, and offer low turnover rates (very little trading), so their fees and tax bills tend to be low as well. Because this type of fund ebbs and flows with the market,

---

[10] https://www.cnbc.com/2017/12/07/self-made-millionaire-tony-robbins-says-to-invest-anything-you-have.html

it stays relatively constant in terms of the stocks that it holds and avoids the risk that comes with picking individual stocks. The trick is not to pick the right company, but to buy all the big companies through the S&P 500 and to do it consistently, and do it in a very, very low-cost way. Index funds also eliminate a major issue that buying individual stocks seems to create, which is ending up with all your money being highly concentrated in one or two positions. You cannot put all your money in one place; it is crucial to diversify your investments. Index funds eliminated the human element, and therefore the risk that is inherent in picking stocks individually by taking a passive approach.

Because humans are not actively managing index funds, they also are not actively making mistakes. When you own an index fund, you're protected against all the downright stupid, mildly misguided, and even simply unlucky decisions that active fund managers are liable to make.

While investment professionals try hard to beat the market, the vast majority fail. Commissions, management fees, short-term thinking, and good old-fashioned analytical mistakes all play a part. Warren Buffett famously made a $1 million bet in 2007 that over a ten-year period, low-cost index funds would outperform hedge funds. He won that bet in 2017. You would be wise to consider this sage advice as you start investing.

Now, that all isn't to say that mutual funds are useless or that it's always a bad idea to buy them. That is just not true. However, it's not a good place to start your investing journey. If you can save $300 a month, and every month buy $300 of an S&P 500 index fund, and just keep doing that consistently for a long period of time, you will end up in a great place. I would say that once you have managed to save and invest to your first $80,000-$100,000 or so, you should consider diversifying your investments.

Since the beginning of the stock market, the best performing portfolio has actually been one that is invested in 80% equities, and 20% bonds, with the portfolio rebalanced to this ratio at the end of each year. Most investors are focused on how to make the greatest amount of money. The smartest financial minds in the world universally want to make money but their first focus is on how to not lose money. If you lose 50% of your money, how much money do you need to get back to even? If you're saying 50%, you're wrong. To get back to even you would have to make back 100%.

The best investors know they cannot be right 100% of the time. Unlike the pundits you see on TV who say "I know for sure what is going to happen," the best investors say, "I don't know exactly what is going to happen. I know what I believe is going to happen. I know for sure I'm going to be wrong at some point, so I need to protect myself through asset allocation, and even if I'm wrong, I'll still do well."

Investing in bonds tends to be a little more complicated than just an index fund. You wouldn't want to invest in a bond index fund. Why? The fixed income markets tend to be more fragmented, and therefore less efficient, than stock markets. The biggest factor is the enormous amount of government debt. Most stock indices weight securities by their market value (share price times number of shares outstanding). An example: Apple has some 6 billion shares outstanding and recently traded at $146.83. Multiply the two numbers and you get its market value of $900 billion. Apple has the highest market capitalization of any U.S. company, and accounts for 3.8% of the S&P 500. A company's stock market value is influenced slightly by how many shares it issues. But the much bigger factor is how popular the stock is with investors. Since going public in 1980, Apple stock has appreciated in value nearly 200-fold.

Bonds are different. Yes, they rise and fall in price, but not nearly as much as stocks do. The price of an investment-grade bond typically does not deviate much from the price on the day it was issued. That means the most important factor in its market value, and thus its weighting in an index fund, is the size of a particular issue. And herein lies the big problem: The federal government is $17 trillion plus in debt. No U.S. company - or companies in aggregate, for that matter - has issued anywhere near $17 trillion worth of bonds. The Vanguard fund, which tracks Barclay's U.S. Aggregate Float Adjusted index, has 65% of its assets in U.S. government debt. The biggest share of that is in Treasury securities, but the fund also has 21% in government-backed mortgage securities. (The float-adjusted index excludes bonds held by the Federal Reserve, which has been trying to depress bond yields and other interest rates through its massive government-bond purchases.) So when you buy the Vanguard index fund or a similar fund sponsored by another firm, you're investing 70% of your money in government debt.

One caveat: Because bond index funds own so much U.S. government debt, where there is little risk of default, these funds should hold up well in financial meltdowns. For instance, in 2008, the Vanguard index fund that tracks the Barclays US Aggregate Bond Index (ticker: VBMFX) returned 5.1%, beating its peers - funds that invest mainly in taxable investment-grade, intermediate-term bonds - by an average of 9.8 percentage points.

The same government-debt issue holds for foreign and global bond index funds. Vanguard Total International Bond Index has 81% of its assets in foreign-government bonds, topped by a 22% weighting in Japanese government securities, whose 10-year bond yields about 0.6%.

The best bet when it comes to investing in bonds? I personally lean toward actively managed and low-cost funds. Vanguard, which I used in this bond index fund example, has several great actively managed funds. Other fund companies, such as Fidelity, Thornburg, Schwab, and iShares all have great options for low cost bond-fund investing.

I generally recommend diversifying as early on as you feel comfortable. Just know that the bond portion of your portfolio is to be used as a buffer to reduce the overall risk in your portfolio. The best investors are obsessed with asymmetrical risk/reward. Most people think billionaires like Ray Dalio took gigantic risks, but when you actually study the best investors, that is not how they operate. They take on the least risk possible for the highest possible return. When it comes to investing, the number one question to ask is: what is the downside?

You will also want to make sure that your investments are tax efficient. You want to structure it so that you maximize your net profits, not your gross profits. It's an ongoing issue with mutual funds since they must sell their holdings and take profits every time that someone pulls out of their funds. Those profits are "mutually" taxed across all investor's portfolios.

Lastly, make sure you don't put all your eggs in one basket. Asset allocation is a science. The best investors in the world want to diversify across asset classes and within asset classes, across markets and economies, and across time.

Make sure your asset allocation truly matches your risk tolerance. This way you will stick it out when markets get bearish, and possibly even choose to invest while everyone is pulling away. That is where the opportunities are. As Warren Buffet famously put it, "be greedy when everyone else is fearful, and be fearful when everyone else is greedy." Every bear market becomes a bull market in the history of the United States. You cannot afford to not be in the marketplace, and you don't want to live in fear because for over two centuries, despite two World Wars and several economic meltdowns, we as a nation keep growing.

Chapter 10

Important Legal Things

"Death is not the end. There remains the litigation over the estate."

— Ambrose Bierce

I am not an attorney, nothing in this writing should be construed as legal advice. Please seek the advice of an attorney for all your legal needs

Estate planning, which is just the coordinating the transfer of your assets through various legal mechanisms, is secretly what gets the inner wheels of my brain working the most. A good estate plan can honestly solve so many problems that I see on an ongoing basis. Let's assume you're too young to have a complicated estate, because this will give me something to write about in the later volumes of this book series. There are a few legal documents that I genuinely think are important for everyone to have in place, or at the very least be aware of and make sure that their parents have them in place. These are:

- Power of Attorney - directs who makes financial decisions on your behalf if you are alive but incapacitated.

- Health Care Proxy/ Health Care Directive - directs who makes health care decisions on your behalf if you are alive but inca-pacitated.

- Living Will - expresses your wishes for life sustaining treatment.

- Last Will & Testament - directs the disposition of your assets upon your death.

Powers of Attorney generally come in two flavors - Durable or Springing. A Durable Power of Attorney immediately appoints someone who can make financial decisions on your behalf - like today (or more accurately, the day the document is executed). This means that whoever you appoint can walk into a bank and request to be added onto your accounts, or withdraw money, or open new accounts, or anything else. They have the financial and legal power to do everything you do. A Springing Power of Attorney gives them the same powers but only if you are incapacitated as verified and signed off by two doctors. There are benefits and downsides to both. I generally recommend that single individuals execute Springing Powers of Attorney, mostly because it likely gives you some semblance of privacy and security that whoever you appoint must jump through some hurdles to make financial changes in your life. On the other hand, the barrier related to springing powers can create a problem when you absolutely want to avoid one.

I had a situation once with a client that is beyond near and dear to my heart, let's call her Mary. When we first began working together, Mary insisted on having a Springing Power of Attorney because she knew her parents were control freaks and she didn't want them monitoring her finances. One day, Mary got into a horrible car accident, and was admitted to the hospital with multiple injuries and in need of several surgeries due to broken bones, impacted nerves, and internal bleeding. A few weeks into her hospital stay, her mom gets a call from Mary's landlord because Mary's rent is past due by over a week! Much to all of our disappointment, because the landlord was a large real-estate management firm, they didn't care too much about Mary's current situation. Mary's mom hurries over to Mary's bank to try and get money out of her account to pay the rent, but the bank will not release it because her mom only has a Springing Power of Attorney. Long story short, amid her daughter having awful and life-threatening surgeries, Mary's mom has to work with doctors at the hospital, and many many many managers at Mary's bank to finally be permitted to make financial decisions on her daughter's behalf.

Fortunately, this story has a happy ending and Mary is off being awesome in all areas of her life! She did make one change though: she switched to having a Durable Power of Attorney in order to make the lives of her loved ones much easier in the event of another incident. You never know when disaster can strike.

For those who are married, I generally recommend Durable Powers of Attorney that appoint the other spouse since you most likely comingle your assets anyway and they are the person easiest to reach in the event you become incapacitated. They are also the person who would likely be responsible for any debt or bills that you have if you died, so you might as well make them responsible while you're alive as well.

There is nothing super specific to mention about a Health Care Proxy/ Health Care Directive except that these are often combined with a living will. Your living will just directs the person who is responsible for making health care decisions on your behalf. Please note that it is absolutely not the same thing as a DNR (Do Not Resuscitate) form that you sign at the hospital. A Living Will does not prevent a doctor from operating on you or bringing you back to life. It is only an instructional tool for your Health Care Proxy.

A "Will" – simple-person-speak for "Last Will & Testament" is a legal document that expresses your wishes regarding the distribution of your property and the care of your minor children, and pets, if applicable. Basically, it ensures that your wishes are followed in the event of your death, takes a lot of the guess work and legal expense out of the equation, and relieves some burden from your children or whoever is left behind once you're gone.

If you don't have a will in place, a court will decide how things are distributed in the event of your death. This means that your loved ones may not receive the assets you wish to leave them. You want your Last Will & Testament to be in writing; Oral wills are not widely recognized from a legal perspective.

Creating a will gives you sole discretion over the distribution of your assets. It lets you decide how your belongings – including cars, jewelry, assets of any kind, clothing, art, and so forth, should be distributed. If you have a business, you can also direct the smooth transition of that as well.

If you have minor children, a will allows you to appoint a guardian for them and allows the guardian to receive compensation for taking care of your children. And last but not least, a will lets you direct your assets to the charity of your choice if you're charitably inclined or in the event you need a good option for a remainder beneficiary (who will receive your assets in the event that all of your family has predeceased you; unlikely... but it does happen).

Things not generally covered by your will:

- Community Property which is usually split based on designation.

- Proceeds from life-insurance policy payouts which have a named beneficiary.

- Retirement account assets which follow beneficiary designations.

- Assets owned as "Joint Tenants with Rights of Survivorship"

- Transfer on death accounts

Basically, anything that already dictates a beneficiary will not go through your will.

The most important thing a will does is provide peace for the family members you leave behind – they don't have to try to figure out, in a time of grieving – exactly what you would have wanted, and most importantly, they will not fight over dishes and nonsense if you have already written out who gets what.

Please ensure that the person who writes your will is a Trusts & Estates (T&E) attorney, not a real estate attorney who happens to write wills on the side. This person should be an active and practicing T&E attorney. Alternatively, if you have relatively simple wishes, you can also use a service like LegalZoom to save some money and create a will yourself.

One other legal document that is becoming more important as time goes on and laws get continuously more complicated is a Revocable Trust.

The greatest benefit of a revocable trust is that it simplifies the estate-planning process. When a person without a trust passes away, the disposition of their property is supervised by a probate court. Not only is this a time-consuming and often costly process, it also generates a public record of the property being passed onto heirs. To elaborate on this, there are certain states where it is particularly crucial to avoid the probate process because it becomes TOO costly and TOO cumbersome to be reasonable. Those people living in Florida, for instance, should do everything possible to ensure they avoid probate. Make sure to do some research to find out how "bad" (costly, time consuming, and inefficient) the probate process is in your state. Probate can be avoided by creating a revocable trust and transferring your assets to it.

Any property transferred to a revocable trust is no longer considered a part of your probate estate. It will pass to your heirs in the manner laid out in the governing trust documents without the need of a court's intervention. This avoids the creation of a publicly available document outlining your assets and their disposition.

Making revocable trusts even more attractive is the ease with which they can be set up. Almost all attorneys that write wills also write Revocable Trusts. The most important thing to keep in mind is that you need to formally transfer the assets to the trust and designate who the trustee and beneficiaries are - in the case of revocable trusts, these are all generally the grantor until he or she passes away, at which point a successor trustee distributes the trust's assets to the residual beneficiaries.

Essentially, while you're alive, the Revocable Trust functions as a personal account with a fancy title. Once you pass, the document directs how your assets are distributed. No one needs to approve it and the trust does not get filed anywhere until your death which also means you can amend your revocable trust as many times as you would like, if you're alive and in good mental health. Upon your passing, your trustee will direct the custodian(s) of your assets on how to distribute your estate based on the instructions written in your Revocable trust.

The net result is this: If you're simply looking for a legal device that will assist your estate-planning process without affording any immediate benefits or protection, then a revocable trust may be the way to go. This is particularly true if you want the flexibility offered by the power to revoke the legal entity. If you also want to protect your assets while you're still alive, and you don't mind relinquishing the right to later change your mind and undo the transfer, then the best course may be an irrevocable trust instead.

There are two downsides to using a revocable trust as opposed to an irrevocable one. First, unlike an irrevocable trust, a revocable trust does not protect the assets therein from the grantor's creditors or legal liability. Because a transfer to an irrevocable trust is, well, irrevocable, its assets are no longer owned by the grantor. Thus, if the grantor incurs a legal liability or owes money to a creditor, those assets cannot be used to satisfy the debt any more than say the assets of the grantor's neighbor.

Second, while a revocable trust allows the assets therein to avoid probate, they are still formally a part of your estate and thus incur estate taxes. Again, just for the sake of comparison, because the assets in an irrevocable trust are no longer yours, they neither go through the probate process nor are they subject to estate taxes.

Be mindful of where you store your estate planning documents. They should be kept in a fire-proof safe somewhere in your home, with additional copies being held in the fire-proof safes of those you appoint to important positions – such as your attorney-in-fact, your health-care proxy, and your executor.

Chapter 11

A Few Tips for Entrepreneurs

"There is nothing more beautiful than someone who goes out of their way to make life beautiful for others."

-Mandy Hale

Financial planning for entrepreneurs and business owners is a bit different than planning for all of us who get paid by an employer. When you own your own business there is no retirement plan already set up for you that you just get to stash money away into. So, if you're an entrepreneur – this one is for you!

Savings options for the self-employed:

Self-directed 401(k)

- You can open one with almost any investment bank and it works the same way as a regular 401(k) except you choose all your investment options and you're the trustee for your own account. It's important to create a good, well-diversified investment portfolio for yourself. This is a solid choice for business owners and their spouses who are able to set aside a significant portion of their earnings. With a solo 401(k), as an employee, you can stash away as much as $19,000 (for 2019). As the employer, you can contribute another 25% of compensation, up to a ceiling of $56,000 for 2019, including your employee contribution. If you're 50 or older,

131

you can toss in another $6,000 extra. Total savings: a whopping $62,000.

- By having a 401(k), you are essentially moving money from one pocket to the other and taking a tax deduction!

SEP IRA (Simplified Employee Pension Individual Retirement Account)

- Simplified employee pension. You set this up for yourself and it's great if you have a few employees too, as you can help them out a bit. You set up the plan with your investment bank and then you have your own account, which you can manage exactly like any other IRA account. The maximum contribution cannot exceed the lessor of 25% of total compensation or $56,000 for 2019. Compensation up to $280,000 in 2019 of an employee's compensation may be considered. Contributions are pre-tax so this is a really easy way to save for retirement if you're a one man show.

- Bonus tip: you don't have to fund the account until you file your tax return.

Defined Benefit Plan

- These usually cost a couple of grand to set up, and are subject to complex Department of Labor regulations, but are so worth it to reduce taxable income especially as you get older. A defined benefit plan is an employer-sponsored retirement plan where employee benefits are computed using a formula that considers several factors, such as length of employment and salary history. Of course, if you're setting this up for yourself and you're the only employee, it works wonders to reduce your taxable income and help you save money for retirement, since you can set up all the rules. This is great for retirement planning and for tax planning.

SIMPLE IRA

- A.K.A. a Savings Incentive Match Plan for Employees. A SIMPLE IRA is designed specifically for small businesses and self-employed individuals. If you have a few employees, say, less than ten who make more than $5,000 per year, but far from six figures, and want to offer a plan for them as a perk, this is probably the one for you. It was designed for firms with no more than 100 employees.

- This one isn't for moonlighters - you cannot contribute if you have already maxed out employee contributions to a 401(k) at your day job. Also, if you need to make a withdrawal from a SIMPLE IRA plan within two years of its inception, the 25% penalty is significantly higher than the 10% fee you would be charged for early withdrawal from a SEP IRA.

Those are the basic ways that you can save for retirement. I would generally advise seeking the counsel of a financial planner to help set all of these up. How you actually retire and leave the business is much trickier than saving for retirement.

Taxes for Small Business Owners

Most of what is written in the Taxes 101 chapter of this book still applies to small business owners, however, there is an important caveat. Small business owners get to claim deductions to their taxable income based on business-related expenses that are incurred throughout the year.

First of all, if you have business expenses please make sure you are paid via a 1099-Form (self-employed) or have set up an LLC or S-corporation through which you can deduct your expenses. Under the new tax law passed at the end of 2017, this is really the only way to deduct those expenses. The entire "Job & miscellaneous deductions" section of the schedule A has been eliminated.

Secondly, there is a business income deduction for small pass-through entities. Most businesses qualify and although certain service businesses (attorneys, accountants, financial advisors, etc.) have an income phase-out, it generally works out beneficially for taxpayers with small businesses. You get an additional 20% deduction on your taxes due, on top of the new lower tax brackets!

Now the fun stuff!

What kinds of expenses can you deduct? Some common ones:

- Marketing expenses
- Home office expenses
- Cost of Goods Sold
- The cost of products or raw materials, including freight
- Storage
- Direct labor costs (including contributions to pensions or annuity plans) for workers who produce the products
- Factory overhead
- Maintenance and repair expenses
- Depreciation and amortization of business assets
- Business start-up costs
- Business car expenses

- Business cell phone/utility expenses

- Insurance costs

- Training/Education expenses

- Retirement plan costs

Unfortunately, those who have business deductions are statistically more likely to get audited – so don't go writing off private jet purchases! Please make sure you track your expenses and have receipts for proof. I'm going to use a yoga instructor as an example for a walk through of how you can significantly reduce the taxes you pay by utilizing expenses!

Let's assume a yoga instructor has an income of $100,000 per year (and files as a single tax payer):

- Income: $100,000

- SEP IRA or 401(k) savings: $6,000

- Adjusted Gross Income: $94,000

- Expenses:

  - Marketing: $2,500

  - Health Plan: $8,000

  - Insurance: $2,000

  - Yoga Mats: $300

  - Blocks/Straps/Tools: $300

  - Cost of Essential Oils for sale: $500

  - Car Expenses: $4,500

  - Gas/Mileage Expense (54.5 cents per mile): $400

- Music/ Subscriptions: $150

- Training/Education/Continuing Ed: $3,000

- Professional Memberships (Yoga Alliance, etc.): $300

- Mandatory subscriptions to maintain licenses: $240

- Yoga apparel for teaching classes: $1,500

- Total Deductible Expenses: $23,690

- Standard Deduction: $12,000

- Taxable Income: $52,342

- Federal Taxes Due Estimate: $17,609 (includes Self-Employment Tax)

- WITH 20% Deduction: $14,087.20

Under the new tax bill your effective tax rate (not counting state taxes) would be only about 20%. If you had a 401(k) and managed to stash away $19,000 (current cap for those under age 50) you could decrease it even more!

Of course, this is all used for illustrative purposes and should absolutely NOT be construed as tax advice. More importantly, make sure to talk to your accountant regarding which retirement plan is best for you and your business.

Chapter 12

How to Pick a Financial Advisor

"Planning is bringing the future into the present, so that you can do something about it now"

- Alan Lakein

I thought it would be helpful and important to put together a list of things to look out for, questions to ask, and information you should know before actually signing an agreement with a financial advisor. Keep in mind that overall you should pick someone that you like, and feel would represent your absolute best interests. This person would ultimately know at least as much about your financial life as you do, if not more, so please make sure you're comfortable with them. Don't feel like you have to keep things from them or might be embarrassed telling them the intimate details of your financial life - that will not serve you in the long run.

The main question you should ask a potential advisor is if they are obligated, by law, to live up to a "Fiduciary Standard" this means that they would be legally obligated to do what is in your best interest, to put your interests ahead of their own, and be able to prove it. The other type of standard that is common is the "Suitability Standard" which basically means that as long as an advisor can convince someone that whatever investments, insurance, or financial planning recommendations they make are "suitable" for you, they are fine. It's the absolute lowest standard and is exceptionally easy to meet.

Generally speaking, you want to make sure someone is legally obligated to do what is in your best interest, and they are not just promising you that they will. The way to do this is to find a Registered Investment Advisor (RIA) to work with. RIA's are registered with the Securities and Exchange Commission (SEC) and created under the laws of the Investment Advisors Act of 1940. RIA's are, by definition, fiduciaries. They are required to implement certain practices and procedures to ensure conformance to the law. At the heart of these is the registration form (ADV Parts I and II) that must be filed every year with the SEC. In ADV Part II, the advisor must disclose all material information a client needs in order to make an informed decision about the advisory relationship or a specific transaction. This includes:

1. All material facts of any instance in which a conflict of interest may exist; past, present or future.

2. Any type of arrangement or relationship the advisor has that could present a conflict of interest, including participation or an interest in any client transaction.

3. All material risks involved with methods of analysis used in determining the appropriateness of an investment.

4. Any unusual risk involved in a specific investment strategy or security.

It will also include general information about the firm, the principals of the firm and their backgrounds, the various advisors and other interested parties, as well as a full disclosure of fees that are charged.

This detailed information must then be compiled into a client brochure and written in clear language and in a specified format so that investors may compare one firm to another as apples-to-apples. Please make sure you ask for a copy of this brochure and try to read through it see what jumps out at you. If it hasn't been provided to you, it's usually on the firm's website, and it's definitely on the SEC website as it is public information.

If, at any point, an advisor is confronted by a client over the appropriateness of an investment, the burden is the with RIA to demonstrate that all measures were taken to disclose the risk, as well as to ascertain suitability. From the perspective of the SEC, documentation is everything. If the SEC were ever to get involved in the investigation of an investor complaint, they require full documentation on the investment strategy used, along with client records that demonstrate knowledge of the client's investment profile and risk tolerance. If anything the advisor says is inconsistent with what is on the ADV, that is a huge red flag.

Next, you will want to ask about the qualifications of the advisor. In many large banking institutions, the only thing an advisor needs in order to work with clients is to pass the Series 7 exam. While it's a great exam to for learning about various investments, especially options, it is not a great qualifier for being able to provide sound financial advice. I've personally seen several "advisors" unable to answer basic tax and estate planning questions because they simply are not qualified to do so and don't have adequate knowledge. It is one thing to be able to plug numbers into financial software and generate an analysis that shows you're 80% or 90% likely to achieve X amount of growth, but they often cannot explain to you what those numbers actually mean to your life. You will want to make sure that they themselves, or someone on their team has a CFP® (CERTIFIED FINANCIAL PLANNER™) designation. If they are providing investment advice, their investment team should also have at least one person with their CFA™ (Chartered Financial Analyst®) designation. There are other credible designations in the industry, such as a CPWA or a ChFC, but you will want to look up what the requirements are for obtaining the designation and make sure that it involves some in-depth study that goes beyond learning how to sell you various products.

You will want to ask them to do some sort of financial planning analysis before you agree to sign on with them, which should go above just investment analysis and advice. Make sure they are able to discuss the implications of your current investments or lack of investments going forward. Ask about the changes they would typically make to your portfolio in the next five, ten, twenty, and thirty years. If you are unwilling to share information with someone and they are willing to bring you on anyway - that is a huge red flag. They should be able to articulate why they need copious amounts of information and they'll likely need to use it all in their discussions with you.

Below is a bare minimum list of documents and information you should be willing and able to provide your Financial Advisor to-be:

- All your current brokerage and bank statements.

- Your tax returns.

- Your employer provided benefits package including details on your retirement plans.

- Detailed information on your family life, your goals, your budget, etc.

- Any and all estate planning documents - Last Will & Testament, any Trusts, Power of Attorney, Health Care Directive, Living Will.

- Any business-related information.

- Any and all insurance information - including life insurance, long-term care insurance, and disability insurance.

A good advisor will continuously request these items until they have all of them because having these makes them able to serve you better. If you're unwilling to provide this information, be prepared to articulate why so that the advisor understands why they might need to create a work around for you.

If you have gotten to the point where an advisor has proposed a portfolio for you, ask detailed questions about what is in it. Make sure you understand the total fees that will be charged to you. Remember that aside from the management fees the advisor will charge you, there are also transaction fees, funds fees, marketing fees, and etc. Make sure you know what you're paying because it will be charged from your portfolio and nothing kills a retirement plan faster than high fees. Some good questions to ask during this time:

- What will change once I have kids?

- What will change when the kids go off to college?

- How will this portfolio change once I'm retired?

- What are all the ways you (the financial advisor) make money?

- Do you get a kick-back from any of the funds or investments that you're recommending?

If the answers are super vague or they basically tell you that changes may be minimal, then that is a red flag. A portfolio should change and evolve as your life changes and evolves.

This may be the most important point of it all: please make sure the person feels good to you. I fully believe that the best people to work with are the people you like. People you would go out to dinner with. People you would trust with your kids. Because ultimately, by handing over your assets to be managed by someone, that is what you're doing. You're trusting them with everything you have and you kids' future. So, if you don't feel comfortable being in their office or they intimidate you in any way, then don't work with them.

I know that trusting someone with your assets is really difficult- especially in the post- 2008/2009 world. But just asking a few questions and really understanding what you're signing up for can save a lot of heartache down the line. A good advisor will be ready, excited, and willing to educate you as much as they possibly can in order to give you comfort.

An advisor that just says "Trust me, I know this, and everything will be okay" is the biggest red flag out there.

Fees

As an Advisor, I often get asked about fees. So, let's discuss all the different types of fees that are likely built into your typical investment account – and yes, you should be concerned and ask about all of them, always.

1. Expense Ratio or Internal Expenses

All underlying investments have some sort of fees associated with them. It costs money to put together a mutual fund, for instance. To pay these costs, mutual funds charge operating expenses. The total cost of the fund is expressed as an expense ratio.

- A fund with an expense ratio of .90% means that for every $1,000 invested, approximately $9 per year will go toward internal expenses in the fund. A fund with an expense ratio of 1.60% means that for every $1,000 invested, approximately $16 per year will go toward internal expenses in the fund.

The expense ratio is not deducted from your account, rather the investment return you receive is already net of the fees.

Example: Think about a mutual fund like a big batch of cookie dough; operating expenses get pinched out of the dough each year. The remaining dough is divided into cookies or shares. The value of each share is slightly less because the fees were already taken out.

2. Investment Management Fees or Investment Advisory Fees

Investment management fees are typically charged as a percentage of the total assets managed. These types of fees may be tax deductible or paid with pre-tax dollars.

Example: An investment advisor who charges 1% means that for every $100,000 invested, you will pay $1,000 per year in advisory fees. This fee is most commonly debited from your account each quarter; in this example, it would be $250 per quarter.

Many advisors or brokerage firms charge fees much higher than 1% per year. In some cases, they are also using high-fee mutual funds in which case you could be paying total fees of 2% or more. It is typical for smaller accounts to pay higher fees (as much as 1.75%) but if you have a larger portfolio size ($1 million or more) and are paying advisory fees in excess of 1%, then you better be getting additional services aside from investment management. These might include comprehensive financial planning, tax planning, estate planning, budgeting assistance, etc.

3. Transaction Fee

Many brokerage accounts charge a transaction fee each time an order to buy or sell a mutual fund or stock is placed. These fees can range from $7.95 per trade to over $50 per trade. If you are investing small amounts of money, or your advisor is "churning" over your portfolio, these fees add up quickly. Churning is a term applied to the practice of a broker conducting excessive trading in a client's account mainly to generate commissions. Churning is an unethical and illegal practice that violates SEC rules and securities laws.

Example: A $50 transaction fee on a $5,000 investment is 1%. A $50 transaction fee on $50,000 is only 0.10%, which is minimal.

4. Front-End Load

In addition to the ongoing operating expenses, an "A share" mutual fund charges a front-end load, or commission. Front-end loads eat heavily into your performance and you should avoid them entirely.

Example: If you were to buy a fund that has a front-end load of 5%, it works like this: you buy shares at $10 per share, but the very next day your shares are only worth $9.50 because 50 cents per share was charged as a front-end load.

5. Back-End Load or Surrender Charge

In addition to the ongoing operating expenses, "B Share" mutual funds charge a back-end load or surrender charge. A back-end load is charged at the time you sell your fund. This fee usually decreases for each successive year you own the fund.

Example: The fund may charge you a 5% back-end load if you sell it in year one, a 4% fee if sold in year two, a 3% fee if sold in year three, and so on.

Variable annuities and index annuities often have hefty surrender charges. This is because these products often pay large commissions up front to the people selling them. If you cash out of the product early the insurance company has to have a way to get back the commissions they already paid. If you own the product long enough, the insurance company recoups its marketing costs over time. Thus, the surrender fee decreases over time.

6. Annual Account Fee or Custodian Fee

Brokerage accounts and mutual fund accounts may charge an annual account fee, which can range from $25 - $90 per year. In the case of retirement accounts such as IRA's, there is usually an annual custodian fee, which covers the IRS reporting that is required on these types of accounts. This fee typically ranges from $10 - $50 per year. Many firms will also charge an account closing fee if you terminate the account. Closing fees may range from $25 - $150 per account. Most of the time, if you are working with a financial advisor that charges a percentage of assets, these annual account fees are waived.

Chapter 13

The Cliff-notes

"There are no shortcuts to true excellence."
- Angela Duckworth

Although I have always believed that there are no shortcuts in life, I understand the value of a quick reference list that you may want to print or rewrite into a planner somewhere so that you have a constant reminder of what you may want to be doing each day to get you closer to your financial goals. The below is a step-by-step quick guide. Please note that this is not meant to be a substitute, for reading all the information in this book.

1. Figure out what you spend. Break this down to fixed expenses and variable expenses.

2. Figure out what you save. This would be everything you are not spending or committed to not spending.

3. Set up a way to automatically pay yourself first. Take your savings directly out of your paycheck each time you get it so that you are saving first, and then spending after.

4. Contribute to your employer's retirement plan savings, or if you're a small business owner, open up your own retirement plan and contribute to it. Try to contribute the maximum allowed by the IRS each year. At the minimum, contribute whatever your employer matches up to.

5. Take care of your credit. Make sure you are not running up a credit card balance and paying high interest.

6. File and pay your taxes in a timely manner each year. Be sure to claim all your deductions.

7. Don't buy life insurance until you need it. When you do, consider buying term insurance, not permanent insurance! If no one financially depends on you, you don't **need** life insurance.

8. Make sure you have adequate disability insurance coverage. Enroll in your employer provided group plan if it's available.

9. Open an investment account. Put your savings into it and buy index funds. The S&P 500 is a good place to start. Diversify as your investments grow.

10. Make sure you have a Power of Attorney, Health Care Proxy, Living will, and Last Will & Testament in place, just in case something happens to you.

11. Hire an amazing financial advisor to help you reach all your goals faster. Making sure they are a fiduciary and are legally obligated to do what is in your best interest.

Chapter 14

Mindset & Conclusion

"The quality of your life equals the quality of your emotions."

— Tony Robbins

I am most certainly not the guru of mindset, please go to a Tony Robbins event to change your life, starting with your mindset. That is my actual and serious advice for you. Attending his event, Date with Destiny, with my husband, not only inspired the completion of this book, but it changed the quality of our daily lives, the quality of our relationship with each other, and our relationships with everyone around us. Tony Robbins is a master at what he does, and his seminars and teachings are incredibly effective for me.

I think it's incredibly important to approach your financial planning with a healthy mindset, which will keep you going when markets are tough, or your life circumstances get tough, or unexpected expenses come into play.

Remember that life is not a competition. Don't think that you can do the same thing your coworker or sibling did with their financial resources and get the same results. You need to create a plan that meets your needs and goals, not anyone else's. A plan that meets your needs, works for you, and that you stick to – that is success. Figuring out what you really want from life and setting up the correct financial planning tools needed to meet that desire will help you create a clear path. Also,

148

if you try to build a financial plan that has you enjoying nothing for ten years, you will not stick with it, no matter the financial planning tools you try. Instead, an honest measurement of where you are now will help you build the plan to financial freedom that actually works. For instance, if you know you enjoy taking a trip each year, account for that. Don't try to convince yourself that you can go without taking a vacation for ten years – that is bad for your bank account and your sense of well-being. Eventually, you will cave and go on an extravagant trip instead of taking a more reasonable getaway annually.

There are many people that have some limiting beliefs about money in general, and most of them are unconscious about it. Have you heard, or even thought, "rich people are greedy", or "money is the root of all evil"? Do you maybe even have one of these beliefs, or something like it? If you have negative associations with being "rich," your chance of achieving the wealth you desire are slim to none, because at an unconscious level, we all move toward the identity that we think is aspirational. Therefore, if you have a negative belief about money and you begin to have some monetary success, you will unconsciously sabotage your success to reinforce your own beliefs. The fact is that capitalism, flawed as it may be, has been a tremendous force for good in the world. A poor person today is infinitely better off than a rich person 100 years ago.

Most of these beliefs were not actively chosen by us, they are a product of our environment or experiences in our formative years. The great news is that you can choose new beliefs for yourself. Mine is: "I'm a force for good". Create an exciting future because it's essential to maintain the vision and hunger necessary to keep going when things are hard. If you're missing a compelling future, you will not use your body and movements effectively. You will not ask good questions. You will

149

come up with language and meanings that sabotage the future you really want. The reality is that the market has a seasonality to it that is predictably unpredictable.

Like the predictability of cold winter storms that show up year after year, market corrections and crashes will continue to rear their ugly heads. We've all suffered losses or know someone who has; maybe it was when the tech bubble burst in the late 1990s, when the stock market plunged in 2001, or when the housing market crashed in 2008. Those kinds of losses can shake you to your core. But the key is to hold on even when the going gets hard. I used the example of Sir John Templeton during World War II, and I would suggest channeling your inner Templeton when you're thinking of bailing on the market when times are tough. Corrections are a regular part of financial seasons, and on average there is one market correction - defined as a decline of 10% or more- per year going back more than a century. Another way to look at it: 80% of corrections are just short breaks during a bull market. Getting scared out of your position means missing more upside.

The truth is that nobody on this planet can accurately predict consistently whether stocks will rise or fall. Warren Buffett once said, "the only value of stock forecasters is to make fortunetellers look good." Just remember that the stock market has always risen, despite short-term setbacks.

The greatest danger is being out of the market. You cannot time the markets, so don't try. Schwab did a study to look at what an investment of $2,000 a year for 20 years starting in 1993 would've returned using three different approaches:

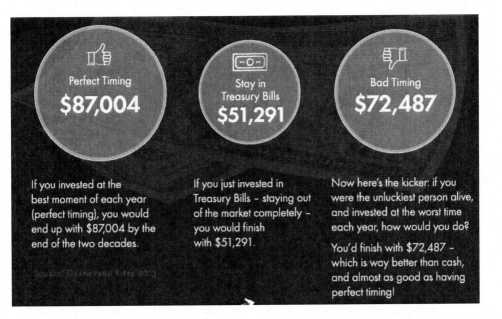

If you invested at the best moment of each year (perfect timing), you would end up with $87,004 by the end of the two decades.

If you just invested in Treasury Bills - staying out of the market completely - you would finish with $51,291.

Now here's the kicker: if you were the unluckiest person alive, and invested at the worst time each year, how would you do?

You'd finish with $72,487 - which is way better than cash, and almost as good as having perfect timing!

What is wealth? There are people that have lots of money, but they are not wealthy, because wealth is really a state of appreciation. If you feel scarcity around money now, you're always going to feel scarcity, no matter how successful you become. Abundance is a mindset, not a dollar amount. Cultivate gratitude for the things you have now and everything that is added will feel like a bonus. Remember that 75% of the world is living on two dollars a day. Your worst financial nightmare is their greatest possible dream.

I need to add in my absolute favorite Tony Robbins quote here:

"You want a formula for wealth? Trade your expectations for appreciation and your entire life changes in that moment. The lack of appreciation is the only thing that will make you truly poor." - Tony Robbins

Conclusion

"Financial fitness is not pipe dream or a state of mind; it's a reality if you are willing to pursue it and embrace it." — Will Robinson

Wow, we've made it to the end here. As I sit here and write this, I cannot help but wonder what you're thinking. Yes, you, the reader. I imagine that you're a close friend of mine, or even family member, and you're thinking about ways you can improve your own financial plan. Or perhaps you're thinking about someone you love in your life and the questions you're going to ask them.

I've kept this book short on purpose. I want it to be something that you can read in about two days. I want financial planning to seem easy and fun for you. I want it to seem like this is no-brainer work for you. I only have one favor to ask: if you learned anything from this book, please pass it on. If you have a high school teacher you're still in touch with, please consider sending them this book so they can share it with their students. Give it to a student that you know.

Perhaps this book has some sparked questions for you, please feel free to reach out to me with any and all of them. I want to help as many people as I possibly can. As an additional note, 10% of all proceeds from this book will go directly towards benefitting a children's education charity, so thank you!

Most of all I just want to say:

I love you

Thank you